FC BARCELONA
A TACTICAL ANALYSIS

ATTACKING
A TEAM FROM ANOTHER PLANET!

WRITTEN BY ATHANASIOS TERZIS

PUBLISHED BY

FC BARCELONA
A TACTICAL ANALYSIS

ATTACKING
A TEAM FROM ANOTHER PLANET!

First Published February 2012 by SoccerTutor.com
Info@soccertutor.com | www.SoccerTutor.com
UK: 0208 1234 007 | US: (305) 767 4443 | ROTW: +44 208 1234 007

ISBN 978-0-9566752-3-1

Author
Athanasios Terzis © 2011

Translation from Greek to English:
Chatzimanoli Eleni

Reviewing the manuscript:
Pardalidou Sofia

Edited by
Alex Fitzgerald - SoccerTutor.com

Cover Design by
Alex Macrides, Think Out Of The Box Ltd.
email: design@thinkootb.com Tel: +44 (0) 208 144 3550

Diagrams
Diagram designs by SoccerTutor.com. All the diagrams in this book have been created using SoccerTutor.com Tactics Manager Software available from **www.SoccerTutor.com**

Note: While every effort has been made to ensure the technical accuracy of the content of this book, neither the author nor publishers can accept any responsibility for any injury or loss sustained as a result of the use of this material.

the Academies of DOXA Dramas (Greek football league, 2nd division).

I wrote and published two books – 4-3-3 the application of the system" and "4-4-2 with diamond in midfield, the application of the system". I decided to proceed in something more specific so coaches would have an idea of how top teams apply the same systems. My next project is the 4-2-3-1 of Mourhinho's Real Madrid.

Analyzing games tactically is a great love and strength of mine. I think teams have success only when they prepare well tactically.

I have watched Barcelona in most of their league and Champions league matches for the last seven years and less frequently over the past twenty years. I believe that this Barcelona side is by far the best Barcelona I have ever seen in regard to their attractive style of play and success in becoming the best side in the world. I have analysed Barcelona's tactics for this book, which together with the teams' incredible technical ability allows Barca to perform their attractive brand of football.

I watched every Barcelona game in the 2010-11 season creating a set of highly detailed notes on each. I watched many of the matches over 20 times. The matches were separated according to the opposing team's formation. This book is made up of over a 1000 hours of

extensive research and analysis of Guardiola's Barcelona side.

Barcelona used a patient passing game, always searching for the opposition's weaknesses. Only if the weak spot of the opponent was found did the team proceed to the final stage of attack.

There were many key tactics, including creating superiority in numbers against the opposition near the sidelines, the attacks through the centre finding an unmarked player behind the opposition's midfielders or using Messi's dribbling skills with driving runs from the right.

Assists were made using vertical passes towards players who made diagonal runs into the box.

Barcelona were able to dominate games by regaining the ball as soon as possession was lost. This was done by retaining the team's balance and cohesion and by having a safety player near the ball (normally Busquets). Combined with Barcelona's ability to retain the ball possession this was the key for dominating the game.

Barcelona have top class players with most being brought up through the youth system, but I believe it is Guardiola's tactics which have defined their success. Previous coaches' have had the same resources, but only Johan Cruyff managed to create a team so tactically fluid and balanced.

Athanasios Terzis

ABOUT THE AUTHOR

ATHANASIOS TERZIS

- **UEFA B coaching licence**
- **M.Sc. certification in coaching and conditioning**

I played soccer for several teams in the third and fourth Greek division. At the age of 29 I stopped playing and focused on studying football coaching.

Since then I have been the head coach of several semi-pro football teams in Greece and worked as a technical director in

TO LENA...

TACTICAL ANALYSIS FORMAT

1. OUTLINE OF THE TACTICAL PHASE OF PLAY

2. PROGRESSIONS WITHIN THE PHASE OF PLAY

3. DIAGRAMS TO SUPPORT THE POSITIONS AND MOVEMENTS
   OF THE PLAYERS

4. ASSESSMENT OF THE PHASE OF PLAY

KEY

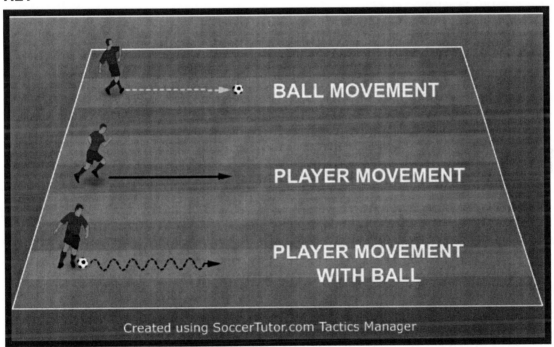

CONTENTS

Introduction 13

Chapter 1 14
The characteristics of Barcelona players 15
• The Player Profiles 16
• Pep Guardiola 20
• 2010/11 Season 4-3-3 System of Play and Player positions 21

Chapter 2 22
The philosophy of Barcelona 23

Chapter 3 24
Barcelona in the four phases of the game 25
• Barcelona in the defensive phase 25
• Barcelona in the transition from attack to defence 26
• Barcelona in the attacking phase 27
• Barcelona in the transition from defence to attack 28

Chapter 4 29
Barcelona in the attacking phase 30
• Positioning: Creating the correct shapes 33
• Movement without the ball 34
• Diagonal Passing 35
• Vertical Passing 37
• Pass and move combinations 40

Chapter 5 43
Barcelona's formation during the attacking phase 44
• Attacking formation 45
• Attacking formation: Variations 46
• Playing with 3 defenders 47
• Creating width 48

The first stage of the attacking phase 49
• Building up play from the back 50
• Vertical pass to the forward 54
• Messi dropping deep into an attacking midfielder's position 56
• Defenders joining the midfield 58
• Switching Positions 60
• Defensive Midfielder's positioning 62
• Movement into Space 64

CONTENTS

• Rhombus/Diamond shape in the Central Zone 66
• Forward dropping deep to maintain possession 68
• Movement: Creating space for others 70
• Using the correct body shape 73
• Maintaining possession from wide positions 75
• Decision making in the final third 77
• Numerical disadvantage in the final third 80
• Numerical superiority 82

Chapter 6 . . . . **.85**
The first stage of the attacking phase against the 4-2-3-1 Formation . . . . **.86**
• Attacking down the flank 87
• Switching play 90
• Receiving with the correct body shape 92
• Exploiting Space 93
• Creating 3 Passing Options 94
• Receiving with your back to goal 96
• Body shape determining the next pass 97
• Approaching the third stage of attack 99
• Central midfield passing options 101
• Maintaining balance in the central zone 103
• Numerical superiority around the ball zone 105
• Wide Forwards 107
• Messi dropping deep 109
• Xavi's options from his central position 111

Chapter 7 . . . .**112**
How Barcelona deal with the opposition's pressing during the first stage of the attacking phase .**113**
• Vertical passes against the 4-4-2 115
• Advancing full backs creating space 116
• Passing out from the goalkeeper 117

Chapter 8 . . . .**127**
Barcelona during the second and third stage of the attacking phase on the right side **128**
• Build up play using a three man defence 129
• Messi's wide movement 131
• Diagonal runs in the final third 132
• Attacking down the flank 134
• Attacking down the flank: Overlapping runs 135
• Combination play near the penalty area 136
• 2 v 2 Attacking down the flank 137

CONTENTS

• 2 v 1 Attacking down the flank 143
• Decision making and maintaining possession 144
• Messi's driving runs from deep 145
• Messi maintaining possession 146
• Messi playing from the right flank 147

The build up play using a two man defence **150**
• Formations 150
• Daniel Alves's passing options 153
• Messi's movement into 'the hole' 154
• Iniesta advancing into Messi's position 156
• Advancing runs from the left back 158
• Messi in the central zone 160
• Switching play 162

Chapter 9 . . . .**163**
Barcelona during the second and the third stage of the attacking phase on the left side **164**
• The build up play using the three man defence 164
• Abidal's passing options 166
• Attacking down the left flank; 2 v 1 169
• Overlapping run 170
• Passing combinations in the final third 171
• One-twos and diagonal runs in the final third 172
• Abidal's passing combinations 173
• Inesta's driving runs 175
• Movement and the final pass 176
• 2 v 2 on the left flank 177
• Maintaining possession in tight areas 179
• Switching the play to the left flank 180

The Build up play using a two man defence **181**
• The left back's passing options 183
• Passing combinations and awareness on the left side 184
• 2 v 1 on the left flank 185
• The left back in an advanced position 186
• Playing out from the back to create a 2 v 1 situation 188
• Awareness and decision making 189
• Vertical pass from the back 190
• Switching from the weak side to the strong side 191
• Decision making: Entering the third stage of attack 192
• Switching play from a central position 196

CONTENTS

• Overlapping runs 197
• Defensive midfielder's passing options 199
• Iniesta attacking down the left flank 200
• Timing runs in behind the defence 202
• Passing through the midfield line 203
• Switching play from left to right 204

Chapter 10 . . . .**205**
The retaining of balance during the attacking phase **206**
• Attacking phase formations; 2-5-3 207
• Attacking phase formations; 3-4-3 209
• Defensive midfielder's role 211
• The full back's role 214
• Maintaining balance; Forwards 216
• Maintaining balance; Left side 218

Chapter 11 . . . .**219**
The transition from attack to defence **220**
• The safety player 221
• Applying immediate pressure when possession is lost 229
• Busquets as the safety player 230
• Using three men at the back 232
• Possession lost near the opposing penalty area 234
• Winning the ball back in the central zone 236
• Regaining possession near the sideline 240
• Regaining possession near to the opponent's penalty area 243
• Cohesion in the transition phase 245
• When immediate regaining of possession is not possible 246
• When immediate regaining of possession is possible 248
• Regaining possession in the centre of the field 249
• Team cohesion to regain possession 250
• Winning the ball in an advanced wide position 253
• The opposition win the ball near the halfway line 255
• Preventing the switch of play 258
• Using two safety players 259

Chapter 12 . . . .**260**
The transition from defence to attack **261**
• Pressing near the sidelines in an advanced position 262
• Transition to the final attacking stage 266
• Intercepting a pass from the goalkeeper 271

CONTENTS

Chapter 13 . . . . **273**
Barcelona's attacking from set pieces **274**
• Corner Kicks 274

Chapter 14 . . . . **277**
• Playing with ten men 278

Conclusion **279**

INTRODUCTION

After the successful 2010-11 season Barcelona could be seen as the best football team of the last twenty years. Other teams have won many trophies but none could reach the outstanding style of play that Barcelona has.

Many people believe this Barcelona side was even better than the team that Johan Cruyff had built in the early 1990's which won four consecutive La Liga titles (1991-1994), a Cup Winner' Cup (1988-89) and a European Champions Cup (1991-92).

Others have compared the team's style of play with that of Zico's Brazil in 1982's World Cup. However this national team of Brazil could not combine the wonderful performances with winning the world cup, while Guardiola's Barcelona won the La Liga title and the Champions League. Barcelona had a spectacular style of play and combined this with highly effective tactics. This book set analyses each one of the four phases of the game.

In the defensive part of this book set we have analysed the way the team applied pressure near to the opposition's penalty area and against teams using different formations (4-4-2, 4-2-3-1, 4-3-2-1 etc), as well as the team's response to tactical situations where the pressing application was not possible.

The defending part of this book set presents the defensive behaviour of the team during situations where the attacking moves of the opposition were being developed, such as near the sidelines and also during the set pieces around Barcelona's penalty area.

During the attacking phase (this book) there is an analysis of the variations of the 4-3-3 formation used by the team, the three stages of the build-up play and how it was (the buildup) done.

The success was driven through the use of effective body shape of the players, the combinations and the movements they usually made on both flanks and in the centre of the field.

In addition there is a chapter which shows how Barcelona maintained their balance in order for the transition from attack to defence to be an easy and successful process.

During the phase of transition from attack to defence every detail of the player's movements in regaining of possession are analysed, as well as the players' actions if the immediate pressure on the ball carrier was not possible.

Finally the book shows the way in which the transition from defence to attack was made and what the aim of the team was (fast break or patient build-up play) as regards to the tactical situation arising on the field.

CHAPTER 1

THE CHARACTERISTICS OF BARCELONA PLAYERS..............................15

THE PLAYERS 16

PEP GUARDIOLA...20

BARCELONA'S FIRST 11 FOR THE 2010-11 SEASON 21
(4-3-3 FORMATION)

THE CHARACTERISTICS OF BARCELONA PLAYERS

If a team wants to be able to perform at their top level by having average possession of up to 70%, using passing combinations in very small spaces and applying pressure to force the opposing team into a passive role, it is certain that the team must consist of top class players.

Only top class players with perfect technical skills and a winning mentality can perform this style of play. Proof of the quality Barcelona's players possess is demonstrated by the fact that eight players out of the starting eleven were crowned champions at the Fifa World Cup 2010 and the other three members of the starting eleven were Messi, Alves and Abidal who are all top quality international footballers.

Barcelona's 2010-11 season was contested with players that were brought up through the youth development program of the club. It was a great achievement having eight players out of the starting eleven coming from the Youth teams of Barcelona. Only Alves, Abidal and Villa were signed from other teams.

If Barcelona had wanted to buy players with the same ability as Messi, Xavi, Iniesta, Pique, Puyol, Valdes, Busquets and Pedro they would have needed to pay extraordinary amounts of money. Barcelona are the best example of building a team though a successful youth training program and an extensive scouting network.

THE PLAYERS

1. GOALKEEPER: VICTOR VALDES

The goalkeeper of Barcelona has very good technical skills, especially in receiving and passing the ball using both feet. This led him to have a significant contribution in the build-up play, something which is very important if a team seeks to dominate the game.

Valdes has high levels of anticipation and great capabilities to read tactical situations and acted as a sweeper coming out of the penalty area. He is also very adept at winning one on ones with the attackers.

Barcelona had the best defensive record in La Liga during the 2010-11 season as the team conceded only 21 goals in 38 matches (0.55 average per game) and kept 19 clean sheets. Victor Valdes had a very important role in the team to produce these astonishing statistics.

2. RIGHT BACK: DANIEL ALVES

A player who never runs out of energy. Because of this fact and his fast transitions from attack to defence, he was capable of covering the entire side of the field, acting as a right midfielder or even as a right forward.

Alves also had the ability to use and create space for his teammates. This led Barcelona to gain a numerical advantage down the flanks and very often Alves was the player who would start the build*up.

During the attacking phase when the team were developing an attacking move from the left, Alves was creating width on the right side. From wide positions mainly, he offered fifteen assists (second best at Barcelona) to his teammates, having a great contribution in the team's attacking play.

22. LEFT BACK: ERIC ABIDAL

Abidal is a tremendous athlete. He was full of energy during the entire ninety minutes showing high levels of speed and strength. He was not making forward runs as often as Alves, but he always had the right timing when he decided to make them. These forward runs would often include overlapping as D. Villa was making driving runs towards the centre or runs inside when Villa was receiving the ball in wide areas down the flank.

Abidal also played successfully as a central defender, replacing Puyol or Pique when necessary. Maxwell and Adriano were both used as left back during the season. They were not as effective as Abidal during the defensive phase, but

they did better during the attacking phase than the Frenchman. The reason for this was their better technical skills that led them to carry out movements in limited spaces and driving runs (especially Maxwell) towards the centre.

5. CENTRAL DEFENDER: CARLOS PUYOL

Very strong player both in the air and on the ground and extremely effective in one on one duels. The captain of Barcelona was adept at taking up positions that allowed him to reach the ball before his direct opponent, both during the defensive phase and the transition phase from attack to defence. He could also defend high up the pitch and close to the midfielders when Barca

needed to press their opponents. Puyol is very accomplished at building up play from the back.

3. CENTRAL DEFENDER: GERARD PIQUE

A very technically skilled and intelligent player. He was extremely comfortable when receiving and passing the ball despite being very tall. He is an ideal defender for a team with the playing style of Barcelona. He has all round talent, because of his ability to defend effectively both in the air and on the ground and also to be involved successfully in the build-up play.

16. DEFENSIVE MIDFIELDER: SERGIO BUSQUETS

The team's key link player. He had great contribution in all the four phases of the game, often doing jobs that the common spectator may not recognise. Without Busquets' contribution, Barcelona wouldn't be able to develop this style of play.

He was disciplined tactically and very good technically. Not in the same level (technically) as Xavi and Iniesta but with great progress from season to season. During the attacking phase, Busquets together with Xavi, was the player who connected the defenders with the forwards, using his passing accuracy and his extended awareness of available options.

Busquet's awareness of teammates' as well as opponents' positioning was provided by the good body shape and great awareness and vision of everything around him before receiving the ball.

During the build-up play he was always taking up the appropriate positions, always being the available player and making the transition from attack to defence easy.

As a result of this the immediate regaining of possession was possible most of the time. If it was not possible, the defensive midfielder's positioning helped the back four to preserve the balance and to cover every free space the opponents attempted to take advantage of.

During the defensive phase, Busquets worked in synchronisation with the two attacking midfielders, both in pressing and non pressing situations.

Mascherano held the role of defensive midfielder in several matches replacing Busquets. He had the same contribution to the defensive phase as Busquets but he was not equally good in participating in the build*up phase. That's why he was not usually one of the first eleven.

6. ATTACKING MIDFIELDER: XAVI HERNANDEZ

Perhaps the most complete player of Barcelona. He can be characterised as the leader of the team, mainly because of his playing position in the field, as his teammates were in the same level as him, as regards to the technical skills and winning mentality.

His fine positioning, his mobility, his vision and the awareness of available options gave Xavi the chance to participate more than anyone in the team's passing game and the build*up from the back. Xavi completed over one hundred passes in several matches in La Liga.

His ability to analyse the tactical situations and to

recognise the positioning of his teammates and opponents quickly and the available free spaces before receiving the ball, led him also to gain extremely high percentage passing accuracy.

Xavi together with Busquets and Iniesta were the three players who dominated possession and dictated the rhythm of the match. However, Xavi's contribution to the defensive phase by taking an active part during pressing situations and his fast transitions from attack to defence were also catalytic in Barcelona's playing style.

He offered seven assists to his teammates and scored three goals. Keita replaced Xavi or Iniesta in several matches. He was better at defensive duties than in the attacking phase and this was the reason he was used as a substitute. This was mainly when the tactical context in the field demanded a midfielder with defensive attributes.

8. ATTACKING MIDFIELDER: ANDRES INIESTA

He is a very flexible player. He was used as an attacking midfielder, as a side attacker or even as a centre forward replacing Messi. His playing style had many similarities to Xavi's as they are both technically skilled, but they had some differences too.

Iniesta would never have the role of the holding midfielder, participating continuously in the passing game. His main role was to take advantage of the free space moving with or without the ball, or to move behind the defensive line in collaboration with Villa and Abidal.

Iniesta's role would be to move near or in the opposition's penalty area more frequently than Xavi and that resulted in more goal scoring chances and more goals for him (eight goals In La Liga).

During the defensive phase Iniesta would get actively involved in all pressing situations and during the transition from attack to defence he reacted very quickly to fight for the immediate regaining of possession.

17. RIGHT FORWARD: PEDRO RODRIGUEZ LEDESMA

He was used on the right side most of the times, but there were several matches that he played as a left sided forward. He started the season impressively and made great progress swapping the Barcelona B squad for the first team.

The basic features of Pedro's playing style are his pace and explosiveness. These features were shown in every move when he used the free space in behind the defence.

Pedro often made diagonal runs towards the centre starting from the right hand side, receiving a final pass from Messi, Iniesta or Xavi.

During the defensive phase, Pedro used up a lot of energy pressing the opposition and during the transition from attack to defence he did not hesitate to put immediate pressure on the new ball carrier.

Having good technical skills especially in moving quickly with the ball, in changing directions and in finishing meant Pedro was able to score a lot of goals (thirteen goals in La Liga and five in the Champions League) along with seven assists. Bojan replaced Pedro in several matches and scored

six goals in La Liga. He did not

have the progression expected, but he was a reliable solution.

7. LEFT FORWARD: DAVID VILLA

David Villa was a great signing for Barcelona during the summer of 2010. He was the player who was missing from Barcelona the previous season. The puzzle had been completed with his arrival in the team.

The team now had the right eleven players to perform the style of football Guardiola wanted. Mainly Villa was used on the left side which was the starting point for his diagonal movements towards the centre of the field.

These diagonal movements were observed by Messi and Xavi and they would utilise many vertical final passes in time of Villa's runs.

On the left hand side he worked in collaboration with Abidal and Iniesta and as the space on this side wasn't as occupied as the space on the right one (when Barcelona used the three man defence during the attacking phase), Villa could take advantage of the free space.

There were also times during the matches where Villa would move into a centre forward's position. The skill set he has suited this position very well as he is blessed with pace, explosiveness and remarkable technical skills.

These features in addition to his killer instinct made him the second (behind Messi) goal scorer of the team scoring eighteen goals in La Liga.

10. CENTRE FORWARD: LIONEL MESSI

Messi has been the best player on the planet in the last few years. He was rewarded as the World Player of the Year for 2009-10. His technical skills were outstanding and he did not hesitate to show them even in very narrow spaces.

He had pace and remarkable explosiveness during his first strides. He preferred making driving runs towards the central zone to moving without the ball. One of his favourite moves was the driving run from the right side towards the opposition's penalty area that usually ended in a vertical or diagonal pass directed to Villa or Iniesta, or a shot at goal.

During the 2009-10 season Messi played as a right side forward. During the 2010-11 season matches he played as a centre forward. However, most of the time he played a role moving close to the midfield zone and towards the right side. This was, as already mentioned, the starting point for his driving runs.

Messi's frequent presence in the midfield zone created superiority in numbers for Barcelona and helped the development of the team's passing game. Because of his strange role in the team Barcelona were characterised as a team without a centre forward.

Messi's quality in finishing led him being the top goal scorer in the team having scored thirty one goals in La Liga and twelve goals in the Champions League.

In addition Messi had great ability in making final passes (assists) as he offered eighteen in La Liga and three in the Champions League. As regards to his contribution to the defensive phase or the transition from attack to defence, it was not as active as the contribution of Pedro or Villa but it was still healthy.

In short Messi was the best of the best.

PEP GUARDIOLA

PLAYER
• **Defensive midfielder, Barcelona 1990-2001**
• **263 appearances (6 goals)**
• **Spain, 47 Caps (5 goals)**
• **Also played for Brescia and Roma**

MANAGER
• **Barcelona B coach, 2007 - 2008**
• **Barcelona Head Coach, 2008 - present**
• **3 La Liga Titles (2009, 2010, 2011)**
• **2 Champions League Titles (2009, 2011)**
• **2 Fifa Club World Cups (2009, 2011)**
• **UEFA Super Cup (2009, 2011)**
• **Supercopa de Espana (2009, 2010, 2011)**
• **Copa Del Ray (2009)**
• **FIFA Ballon d'Or - Coach of the Year Award 2011**

As a player, Pep Guardiola was part of Johan Cruyff's team which was the first Barcelona side to win the European Cup (1992). The influence Cruyff has had on his managerial style is very clear to see.

After Guardiola had retired, his first managerial post was with the Barcelona B side where he did extremely well and was appointed head coach of the full Barca side for the following season.

He has had unbelievable success, winning 13 of a possible 16 trophies.

Pep took over as head coach of the Barca team in 2008 at the age of 37 and led the side to the first treble in Spanish football history (La Liga, Champions League and Copa del Ray).

• **In 2009 Barca won all 6 of the competitions they were in after they added the Supercopa,** the UEFA Super Cup and the Fifa Club World Cup.
• **In 2010 Barcelona won the La Liga title and the Supercopa de Espana.**
• **In 2011 Barca won La Liga, the Champions League, Fifa World Club Cup, UEFA Super Cup and the Supercopa.**

Barcelona have always been one of the biggest clubs in the world, but Pep Guardiola has probably shaped the best football team in history, both with their style and their success in winning trophies. All the Barca players have a very high technical level, but it is Guardiola's extensive tactics which create the incredible cohesion and fluidity to this Barcelona side. As head coach, Guardiola gets his players to play free-flowing attacking football but also instills a defensive responsibility into all of them.

Many Barcelona coaches have been highly successful but Guardiola's rate of winning 13 trophies out of 16 is unmatched anywhere.

BARCELONA'S FIRST 11

FOR THE 2010-11 SEASON (4-3-3 FORMATION)

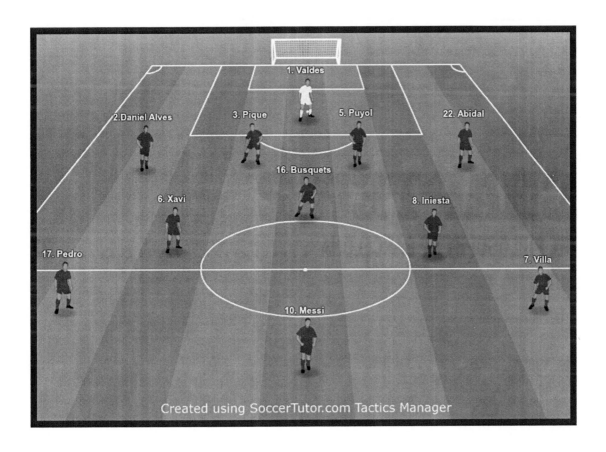

CHAPTER 2

THE PHILOSOPHY OF BARCELONA 23

THE PHILOSOPHY OF BARCELONA

Throughout Barcelona's history they have been under the charge of great coaches with an obvious preference to those who came from Holland.

The Dutch coaches who took charge of Barcelona were Rinus Michels (awarded as the best coach of the century), Johan Cruyff, Luis Van Gaal and Frank Rijkaard. All of them had something in common as they had all coached at Ajax Amsterdam in the past.

Barcelona have been heavily influenced by the Dutch (Ajax's) playing style, not only because of the managers, but also because of the several Dutch players who played for the club for the previous thirty to forty years.

FC Barcelona's current set up was built with Ajax as the model. Barcelona developed a youth training program in order to bring through more players from its Academy. All of the young players worked systematically improving specific technical and tactical skills and collectively the youth teams were preparing to apply the 4-3-3 formation or they were using it already.

The application of 4-3-3 was based on dominating the game by dictating possession in the opposition's half of the field by pressing high up the pitch and trying to regain possession as soon as possible after the ball was lost.

The club also worked hard to set up a scouting network to track young players all around the world who had the qualities to join Barcelona's youth teams.

Years of hard work passed by before the team managed to reach the top of Europe (season 2010-11) having eight players out of the starting eleven coming from the Barcelona youth system, an incredible achievement.

CHAPTER 3

BARCELONA IN THE FOUR PHASES OF THE GAME

• Barcelona in the defensive phase 25

• Barcelona in the transition from attack to defence..26

• Barcelona in the attacking phase 27

• Barcelona in transition from defence to attack 28

BARCELONA IN THE FOUR PHASES OF THE GAME

BARCELONA IN THE DEFENSIVE PHASE:

When Barcelona were not in possession of the ball their aim was to regain it as soon as possible and often near to the opponent's penalty area by applying pressure.

Many teams during this phase prefer to sit back in a zone near the halfway line and wait for the opponents to come. These tactics usually lead them to having plenty of free space to use when they regain possession. However, Barcelona reached very high standards of retaining possession in very small spaces and are capable of unlocking even the best and most organised defences.

Barcelona did not need to use these kinds of tactics due to their immaculate technical level.

BARCELONA IN THE TRANSITION FROM ATTACK TO DEFENCE

As soon as Barcelona lost possession their main aim was to immediately put pressure on the new ball carrier. This would either result in the direct regaining of possession or the indirect by forcing the player into an unsuccessful pass. During this phase the free player had a very important role and in most of the situations this was the defensive midfielder Sergio Busquets.

Many said that the strength of Barcelona was their ability to retain possession and to search patiently for the weaknesses of the opposition.

However, the way Barcelona functioned during this transition phase was equally as strong. The constant psychological pressure that was put on the opposition by trying to regain possession as soon as possible after losing it, made Barcelona's domination easier to achieve.

When the loss of possession took place in the centre of the field and the immediate turnover of possession was not possible (there were not any Barcelona players near the ball zone to put pressure) the main aim of the team was to prevent the vertical and diagonal passes. This was done by tracking back and building a wall that forced the ball carrier to make square passes. By this action the ball was directed towards the sidelines where the application of pressing was possible again.

When the loss of possession was taking place near the sidelines and the direct pressure on the ball carrier was not possible, the team (lead by the defensive midfielder) would squeeze the play and aim to keep the ball in the same zone to make the opposition's attacking move predictable and give time to the rest of Barcelona's players to fully recover.

Barcelona's function during this phase was perfect. This was the reason that every opposing team had great difficulties in taking advantage of the free spaces behind the defence that Barcelona's playing style created.

The players' consistency in doing their jobs during this phase of transition led the team to have La Liga's best defensive record.

BARCELONA IN THE ATTACKING PHASE

When Barcelona had possession it was wonderful to watch. Having high quality players the team could retain possession making over thirty passes in a row. The basic aim was not to rush during the build-up play, but to search with patience for the weaknesses of the opposition and then carry out the final stage of the attacking phase.

The final stage of the build-up could take place on the right side, on the left side or in the centre of the field with the same frequency. Very important elements of the team play during this phase were:

a) The creation of superiority in numbers near the ball zone and especially on the right part of the field, where Messi was moving to meet the ball.

b) The creation of ideal formations (triangles and rhombus).

c) Maintaining width with the forward and full back's runs.

d) Maintaining a compact team unit by synchronizing the movement of all the players.

e) The use of diagonal passes during the first and the second stage of build-up and the use of vertical passes during the final (third) stage as well as the use of combination play in order to create and use the free spaces such as give and go, one – two's, cutting and overlapping.

BARCELONA IN TRANSITION FROM DEFENCE TO ATTACK

The transition from defence to attack was very quick. The team's playing style of dictating possession in the opposition's half meant the opposition were compact and well organised defensively having ten players behind the line of the ball most of the time. This meant that the positive transition usually had the form of eleven against eleven play.

If the regaining of possession was taking place in a part of the field where many opponents were above the line of the ball, the team was trying to play out its attacking action with speed using vertical or diagonal passes and taking advantage of the forwards' pace.

The direct fast breaks were formed as follows:

There would be a diagonal move in behind the defence from one or both of the wide forwards (Pedro and Villa) and at the right moment Xavi, Iniesta or Messi made the final vertical pass.

For the times that the direct fast break was not possible, often when the opposing team had closed the angle for available vertical passes, the ball carrier would use a diagonal pass directed to the forward that had stayed wide near the sideline. Then there would be a run inside and beyond the defensive line from one of the attacking midfielders (usually Iniesta) or one of the full backs (usually Alves).

CHAPTER 4

BARCELONA IN THE ATTACKING PHASE

. Positioning: Creating the correct shapes 33

. Movement without the ball 34

. Diagonal passing 35

. Vertical passing 37

. Pass and move combinations 40

BARCELONA DURING THE ATTACKING PHASE

When Barcelona played against an opponent, the most spectacular part of the game to watch was Barcelona's play during the attacking phase. The way the team perform during this phase is the reason why Barcelona have millions of fans from all around the world and are the most popular team on the planet.

The attacking phase includes all the team's actions as soon as they have possession of the ball, with the aim of scoring a goal. This can be separated into three stages:

The first stage:
Includes all the actions taken to move the ball from the defenders to the midfielders (passing game using mainly diagonal and vertical passes).

The second stage:
Includes all the actions taken (passing game using diagonal and vertical passes and creating numerical superiority down the flanks with driving runs) mainly by the midfielders but also by the forwards or even by some of the defenders of the team.
The aim of this phase is to to move the ball to positions where the final pass towards the attacking players is easy (on the flanks or behind the opposition midfield).

The third stage:
Includes the final pass/assist (diagonal or vertical) or the low cross into the box towards the attacking players and the final shot/header on goal.
The build-up play during the attacking phase not only starts when the goalkeeper has the ball, but also when the regaining of possession is achieved.

Depending on the part of the field that the regaining of possession takes place, some of the stages of the attacking phase can be skipped.

There are teams which prefer to get from the first stage directly to the third by using long passes from the defenders straight to the forwards. This way of playing is the opposite of Barcelona's philosophy and rarely takes place in games.

The main element of Barcelona's play during the attacking phase is their ability to dominate the game for the full 90 minutes. This domination was a result of the extremely high possession percentages, the high tempo of the game and the ability of the team to win the ball back immediately after losing it.

Barcelona progressed through the three stages of the attacking phase by patiently passing the ball, reaching the second phase and going back to the first as many times as necessary to find the right time to move on to the third stage.

The passing game the team used included many diagonal and vertical passes and restrained the opposing team to a passive role on the game.

Barcelona used their passing game together with the driving runs of Messi on the right side and those of Iniesta's or Villa's on the left, to break down the opponent's first line of defence (made up of the forwards and the midfielders).

As soon as this block was broken down, a free final pass (assist) towards the attacking players could be achieved (diagram 49, A area - shown on the next page).

When players reached the A area, the build up progressed to the third stage, which included a diagonal or vertical pass towards the attacking players, who have moved into the box, having made vertical or diagonal runs.

In situations where the build up play was taking place on the flanks, Barcelona's aim was to create superiority in numbers and then use this favourable situation to move the ball in behind the opposition's defensive line.

The numerical superiority on the right side was achieved with Alves' forward runs and his collaboration with Pedro, Xavi and Messi, while on the left side there were combinations between Villa and Iniesta with the forward runs of Abibal or Maxwell/Adriano.

The third stage on the flanks included low crosses from the side of the penalty area directed to the attacking players moving inside the box (diagram 49, B area).

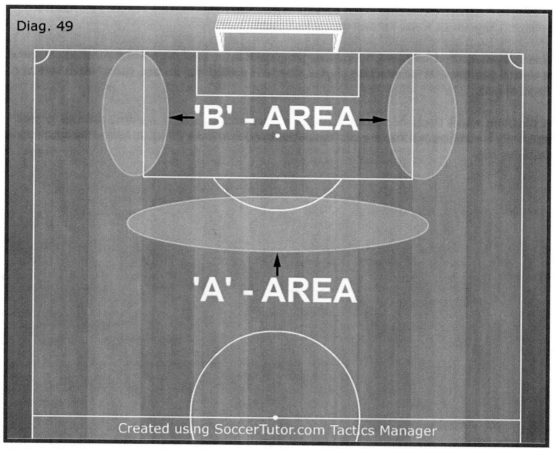

Diag. 49

'B' - AREA

'A' - AREA

Created using SoccerTutor.com Tactics Manager

Watching Barcelona during their attacking phase highlights their creativity, their combinations in very small spaces, their technical quality and their domination of possession.

Many would thus conclude that Barcelona's play is very complicated.

However, this is not the right conclusion.

Taking into consideration the perfect technical ability of the players, the spectacular results of their attacking play comes from a simple passing game using diagonal and vertical passes, together with the correct positioning and intelligent movement without the ball.

POSITIONING: CREATING THE CORRECT SHAPES

For the development of the attacking play with diagonal and vertical passes, it is necessary for the players to create the right shapes.

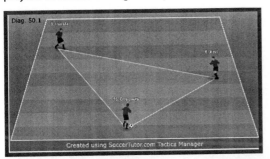

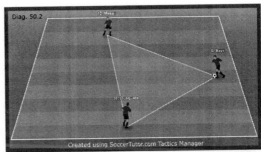

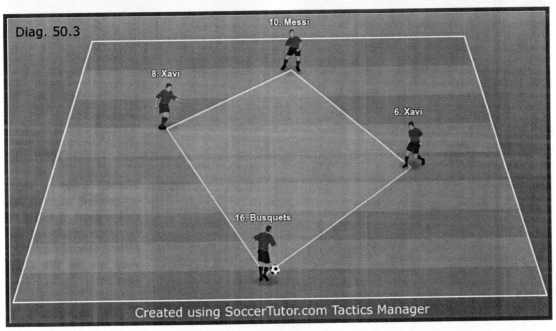

These shapes shown are the triangle and the rhombus (diamond/angled type shapes), the creation of which are clearly shown during Barcelona's attacking play (diagrams 50.1, 50.2 and 50.3).

MOVEMENT WITHOUT THE BALL

When the term right positioning is used, it means the players must be in the appropriate place in order to create the correct angles and shapes to favour the diagonal or vertical passes.

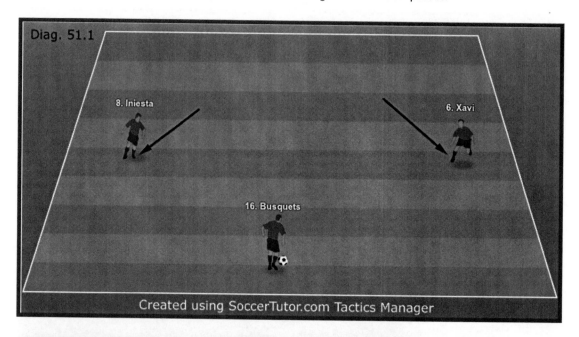

When the term movement without the ball is used, it refers to the runs made by the players to make sure they are in the right position.

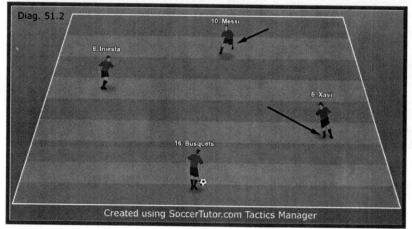

If the movement is correct the right shapes are created and the available passing options are increased (diagrams 51.1 and 51.2).

DIAGONAL PASSING

When the right positioning of the players and the movement without the ball is provided, diagonal passes come naturally. These kinds of passes are used by Barcelona's players for two reasons:

1) They ensure safety if the ball possession is lost.

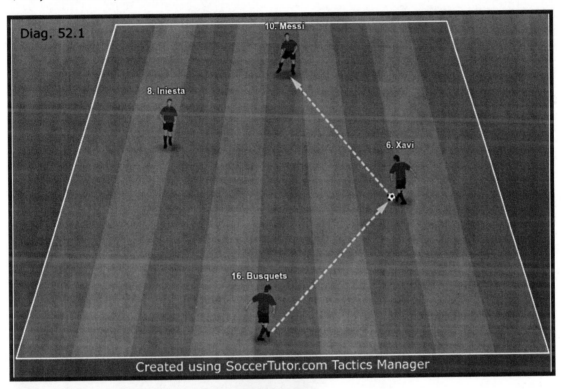

Diag. 52.1

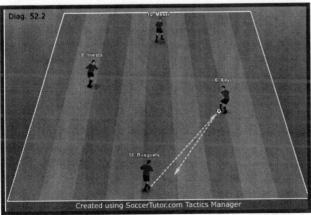

b) They provide more available options for the new ball carrier, as he has the possibility to pass forward or back (diagrams 52.1 and 52.2)

Diag. 52.3

10. Messi

8. Iniesta

6. Xavi

16. Busquets

Created using SoccerTutor.com Tactics Manager

The player can also move forward with the ball (diagram 52.3).

The players who take up positions to receive a diagonal pass usually have the proper body shape and positioning, which enables them to have awareness of the available options (diagrams 52.1, 52.2, 52.3).

All of these elements shown are necessary for Barcelona's effective passing game.

VERTICAL PASSING

Vertical passes are used a great deal during the attacking phase of Barcelona.

Their importance can be seen in the fact that when they are used, they can pull a lot of players out of defensive positions, especially when used in the first stage of the attacking play.

Diag. 53.1

Barcelona did not have a centre forward who would play with his back to goal, who could use strength and power.

Instead the team would play to their strengths when receiving a vertical pass.

Players such as Villa, Messi and Pedro are quick with great technique so the forwards would make either a pass backwards and then move without the ball to stretch the defence.

Or, would receive and move with the ball, pass, and then move without the ball.

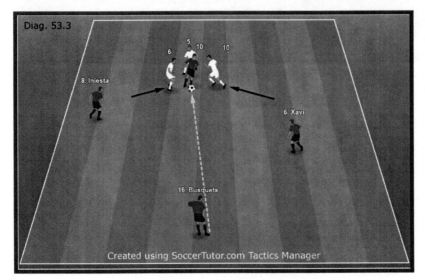

With these combinations the ball was kept moving. Possible double marking by the opponents could be avoided (diagram 53.3) and the passes were directed to players who had the proper body shape to receive.

It must be mentioned that the use of vertical passes during the last stage of the attacking play was very effective.

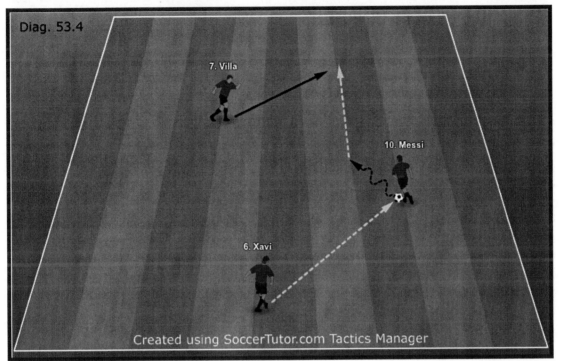

During the third stage the ability of Barcelona players, such as Messi, Iniesta and Xavi, in combination with the diagonal movements of Villa or Pedro firstly (diagram 53.4) and Messi, Iniesta and Xavi secondly, made Barcelona unstoppable.

PASS AND MOVE COMBINATIONS

Finally, a very important element of the team's attacking play which helped Barca retain the ball for a great deal of time, were the pass and move combinations used by all Barcelona players. The movement after passing the ball was usually in one of two directions.

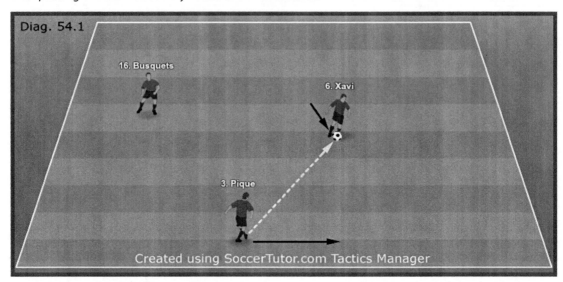

Firstly, there was a pass followed by a movement to give support behind the ball, which was used when the defenders combined with the midfielders (Diagram 54.1).

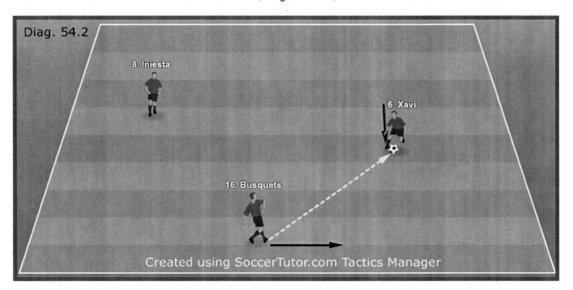

Secondly, between the midfielders (Diagram 54.2).

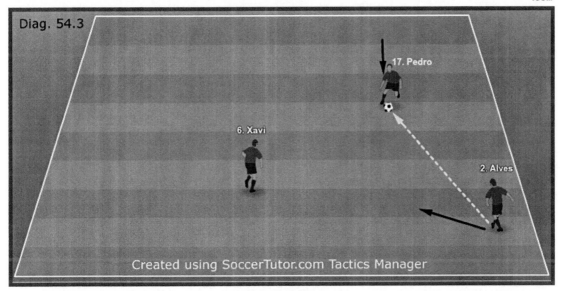

Diag. 54.3

And finally, the full backs with the wide forwards (Diagram 54.3).

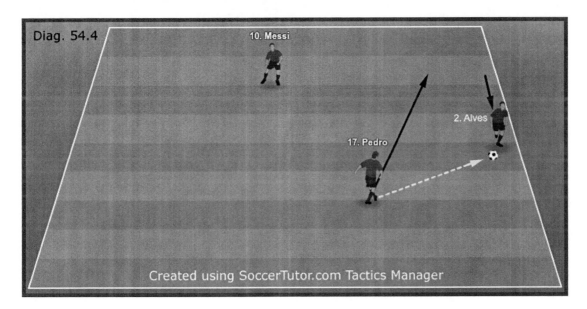

Diag. 54.4

There were also passes followed by a movement to attack space or create space.

This was often shown with combinations between the wide forwards and the full backs when they were in advanced positions (Diagram 54.4).

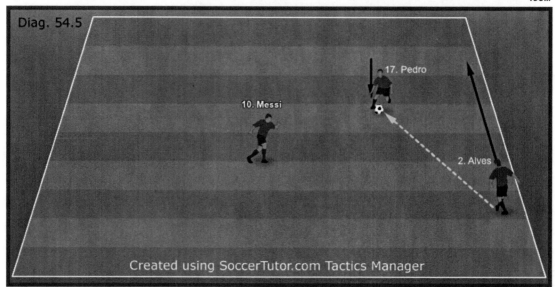

Many Barcelona players would also use overlaps (Alves & Pedro, diagram 54.5).

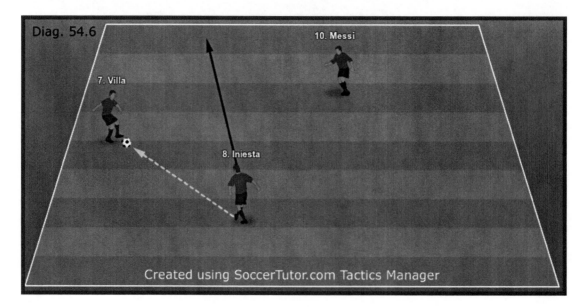

Even the attacking midfielders would use this combination with the wide forwards (Iniesta & Villa, diagram 54.6).

CHAPTER 5

BARCELONA'S FORMATION DURING THE ATTACKING PHASE

- **Attacking formation**..**45**
- **Attacking formation: Variations**...**46**
- **Playing with 3 defenders** **47**
- **Creating width** **48**

THE FIRST STAGE OF THE ATTACKING PHASE

- **Building up play from the back** **50**
- **Vertical pass to the forward**..**54**
- **Messi dropping into an attacking midfielder's position** **56**
- **Defenders joining the midfield** **58**
- **Switching Positions** **60**
- **Defensive Midfielder's positioning** **62**
- **Movement into Space** **64**
- **Rhombus/Diamond shape in the Central Zone** **66**
- **Forward dropping deep to maintain possession**...**68**
- **Movement: Creating space for others** **70**
- **Using the correct body shape** **73**
- **Maintaining possession from wide positions** **75**
- **Decision making in the final third**..**77**
- **Numerical disadvantage in the final third**..**80**
- **Numerical superiority** **82**

BARCELONA'S FORMATIONS DURING THE ATTACKING PHASE

It is widely known that Barcelona for many years, because of their strong Dutch influence use the 4-3-3 formation. Guardiola's side normally had Pedro and Villa as the wide forwards and the centre forward was usually Messi. They are seen to always use the 4-3-3 formation but this is not completely accurate.

During the defensive phase Barcelona would use the 4-3-3. Messi would take up a position near the edge of the opponent's penalty area and put pressure on the opponents' central defenders.

When Barca had possession and the build up was in action, the team used one of two different formations.

The formation used during the attacking phase changed depending on the number of opponent forwards. Barcelona always wanted to have a spare man at the back. So when the team faced an opponent who used two forwards, the main aim of Barcelona was to ensure numerical superiority with three defenders against two forwards.

There were cases against teams that used two forwards, the temporary three man defence was composed of the two central defenders and the left back (Pique, Puyol, Abidal), or Busquets would use deeper positioning close to the two central defenders, allowing the two full backs to move forward. This was when a more attacking left back was playing, such as Maxwell.

When the opposition used only one forward, the defensive midfielder could move further up the field and give support to the attacking midfielders so the team could win the ball back immediately if possession was lost. In defence there was a situation of two Barca defenders against one forward.

Lionel Messi would often drop back into an attacking midfielder's position providing numerical superiority in the central zone and an extra passing option not only for the midfielders but also for the defenders of the team. In this way the passing game could be developed and the ball could easily be directed to the forwards. The positioning of Messi deep in midfield was the reason that the formation of Barcelona was called the formation without a centre forward.

ATTACKING FORMATION

Diagram 55.1 shows the formation used in the attacking phase when Alves and Abidal were the two full backs.

Alves was usually moving forward taking up positions in midfield, while Abidal stayed back with the two central defenders.

The attacking width was provided by Alves' forward runs on the right and by the positioning of Villa near the sideline on the left.

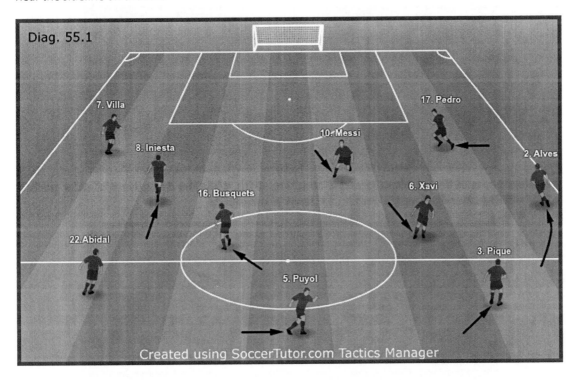

Diag. 55.1

The defensive midfielder (Busquets or Mascherano) worked closely to the two attacking midfielders when the ball possession was lost in order to win the ball back immediately.

In defence there would be a numerical superiority in favour of Barcelona (usually 3v2).

ATTACKING FORMATION: VARIATIONS

When the two full backs were Alves and Maxwell/Adriano and Barcelona were facing a team using two forwards, the formation used was the one which is shown on diagram 55.2.

Diag. 55.2

The forward runs of the full backs provided attacking width, while the defensive midfielder worked closely with the central defenders creating a numerical superiority.

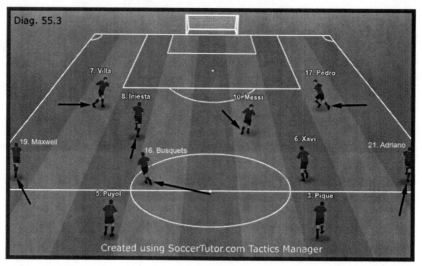

Diag. 55.3

If the opponents used one forward, then the formation of Barcelona was changed into the one shown on diagram 55.3, with the defensive midfielder moving slightly towards the left side and Iniesta moving up to a more advanced position.

PLAYING WITH 3 DEFENDERS

During the 2010-11 season, the central defenders were often joined by a full back to create a formation with 3 at the back.

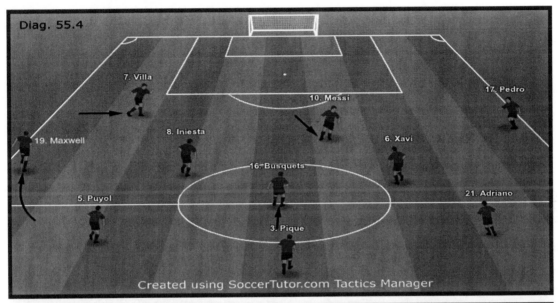

Diag. 55.4

Created using SoccerTutor.com Tactics Manager

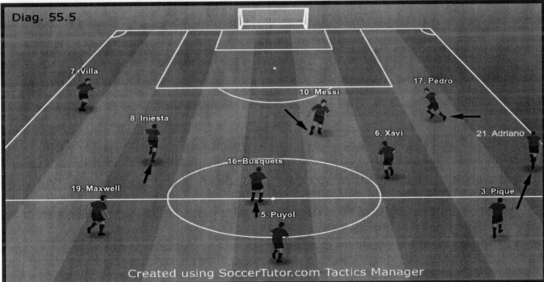

Diag. 55.5

Created using SoccerTutor.com Tactics Manager

The new tactical situation meant that Busquets could push up and give support to the other midfielders (diagrams 55.4 and 55.5).

CREATING WIDTH

Finally there were times that the defensive midfielder dropped very deep and took up a central defender's position.

The 2 central defenders would push out wider allowing the full backs to move higher up the pitch.

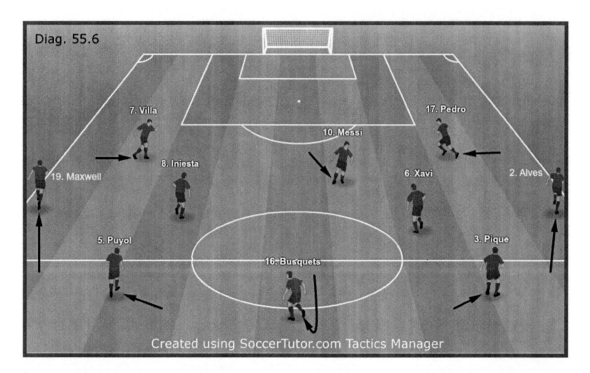

This formation was used in two situations:

1. When the opposing team was compact in the centre of the field limiting the available space.

2. When the opposition forwards would work close to each other.

When these two situations occurred it was far more difficult to move the ball from the defenders to the midfielders through the central of the pitch.

This formation provided even more attacking width and favoured the build up play from the back and down the flanks.

THE FIRST STAGE OF THE ATTACKING PHASE

Barcelona traditionally build up play from the back, using a patient passing game.

The defenders of the team are heavily involved in the attacking phase.

Their main aim is to break down the opponent's pressure using short passes. Only when there were not any available short passing options did the team use long passes.

Diagrams 56.1 up to 56.2.1 show Barcelona with Alves and Abidal in the first eleven with the opposition using the 4-4-2 formation.

The use of this formation favoured attacking from the right side rather than the left. The frequent build up play on the right resulted in three factors:

a) The frequent forward runs of Alves, who used to take up positions high up the field, creating space on this side for Pique, Xavi, Messi and Pedro to use.

b) The positioning of Xavi towards this side, who was the player who dictated the team's passing game and rhythm.

c) The outnumbering of the opposition in the midfield, caused by Messi's deep position.

Additionally, the opponent who had to track Alves during his runs left the opposing team with only three players in midfield. The remaining 3 then had great difficulties to cover the entire width of the field.

BUILDING UP PLAY FROM THE BACK

Diagrams 56.1 and 56.1.1.

Alves moves up and creates space while the white No.11 tracks him. Pique, after receiving the ball takes advantage of the space by pushing up.

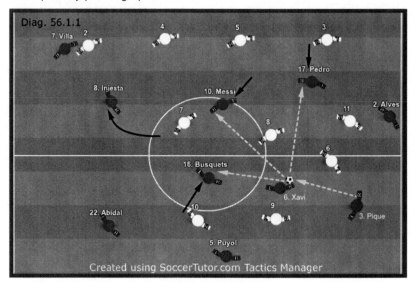

The white No.6 moves to put pressure on Pique. Xavi drops back and receives the ball while being free of marking. His available options are shown on diagram 56.1.1.

EXAMPLE 2

On diagram 56.2, No.9 tracks Pique and tries to close him down.

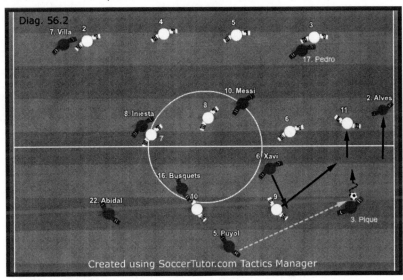

Xavi drops further back to receive the ball free of marking once again.

When No.6 seeks to follow Xavi's movement he will leave a gap in midfield.

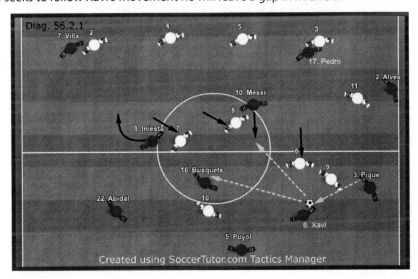

Xavi's possible passing options are shown on diagram 56.2.1.

EXAMPLE 3

On diagrams 56.3 and 56.3.1 Barcelona are playing out from the back again.

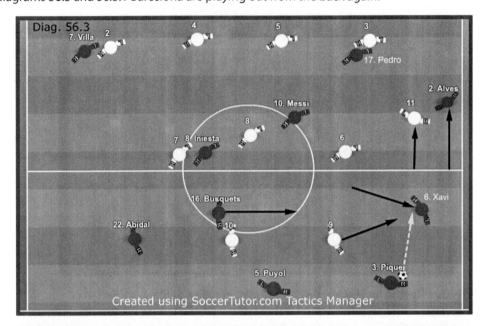

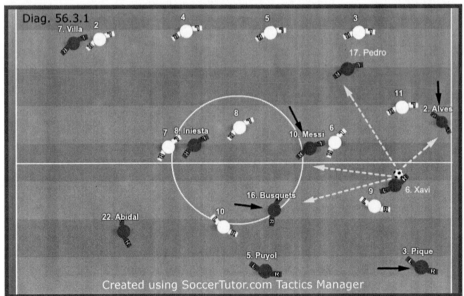

Xavi makes a movement to receive near the side line and still has four good options to pass the ball.

EXAMPLE 4

Diagram 56.4 shows the attempt of the white team to keep the ball near the right side line.

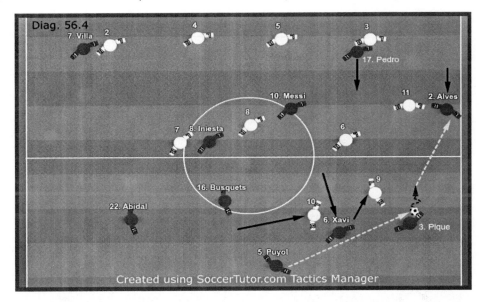

Pique moves forward and Xavi drops back but he is under No.10's marking. So the ball carrier has only two available options which are Alves and Pedro, who move to receive.

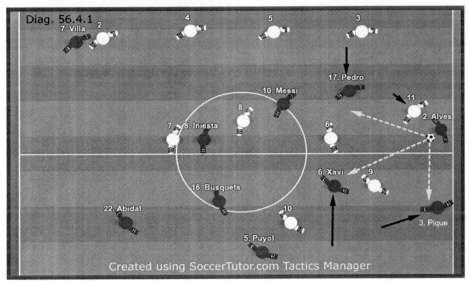

Barcelona break down the pressure because of their players' mobility, who after Pique's pass to Alves move into positions providing support for the new ball carrier (diagram 56.4.1).

VERTICAL PASS TO THE FORWARD

On diagram 56.5, the ball carrier (Pique) passes the ball to Pedro.

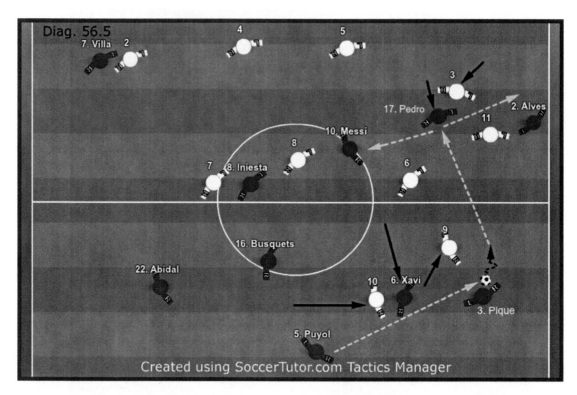

Pedro receives and due to the white team's positioning, he has the options to pass the ball to Messi or Alves and the team can proceed to the final stage.

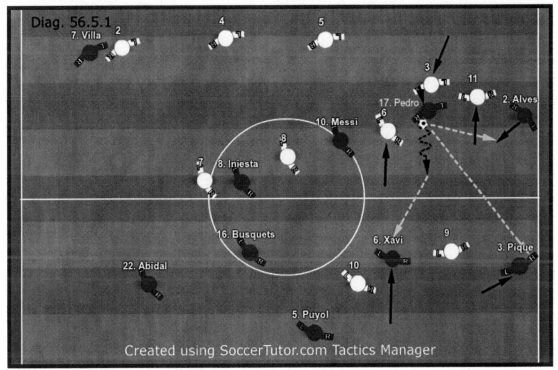

Diag. 56.5.1

Created using SoccerTutor.com Tactics Manager

On diagram 56.5.1, we show the same scenario.

This time the white team responds differently and blocks off the passing angles towards Messi and Alves.

As there are no possibilities for the team to directly reach the final stage, Barcelona can only retain the ball possession with Pedro passing towards Xavi, Pique or Alves who have all moved into positions to receive.

 ASSESSMENT

Pique bypasses the midfield to pass straight to a forward, skipping the first stage.

The decision of whether to try to enter the final stage or pass backwards was always determined by the positioning of the opposition defenders.

MESSI DROPPING INTO AN ATTACKING MIDFIELDER'S POSITION

Diagrams 56.6 and 56.6.1.

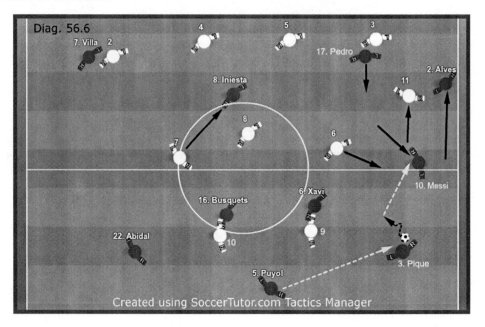

Here we show the movement of Messi towards the sideline into the free space created by Alves.

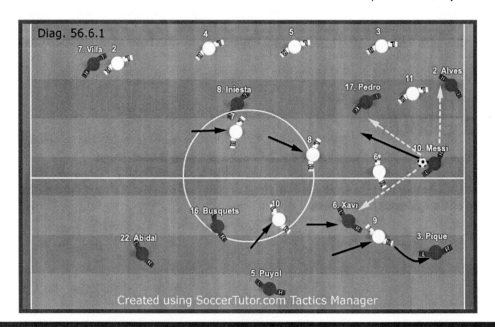

The right side favoured the left footed player (Messi) to make his driving runs.

Every time there was a big enough gap between the opponent's midfield and defensive line, Messi used his ability to dribble the ball even when he had limited space to play in.

 ## ASSESSMENT

Alves' freedom to attack in this formation is shown well here, as his advanced position creates space for his teammate to exploit.

This is possible because Barca played with 3 defenders.

DEFENDERS JOINING THE MIDFIELD

Diagrams 56.7 and 56.7.1.

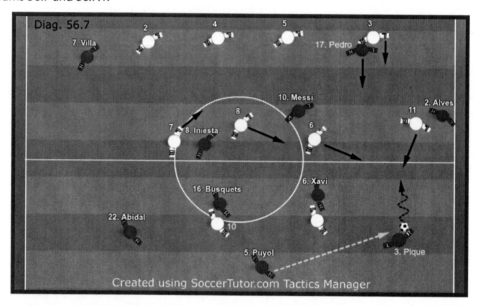

The white No.11 closes down Pique who runs forward with the ball.

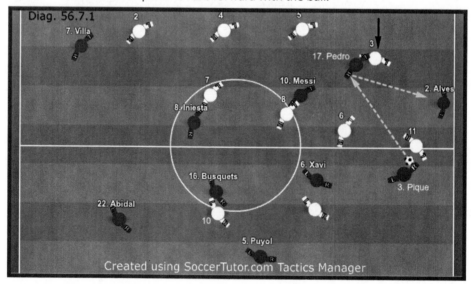

Pedro makes a movement to receive and the ball is directed to Alves through him.

 ASSESSMENT

Xavi and Busquets deep positions provide security so Pique can push forwards and play out from the back.

SWITCHING POSITIONS

Diagrams 56.8 and 56.8.1.

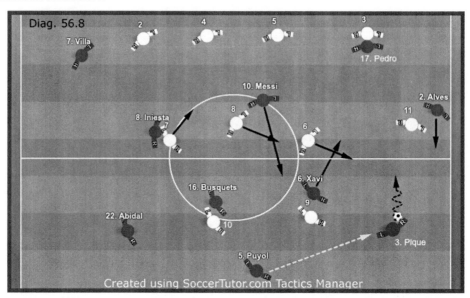

Xavi moves forward to give support to Pique ahead of the ball, while Messi drops back in a coordinated movement between the two players.

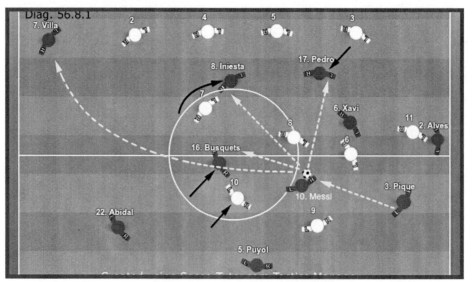

Messi receives the ball and the other Barcelona players move to provide support for him.

ASSESSMENT

Barcelona are an extremely fluid team, able to change positions frequently to maintain possession.

DEFENSIVE MIDFIELDER'S POSITIONING

Diagrams 56.9 and 56.9.1.

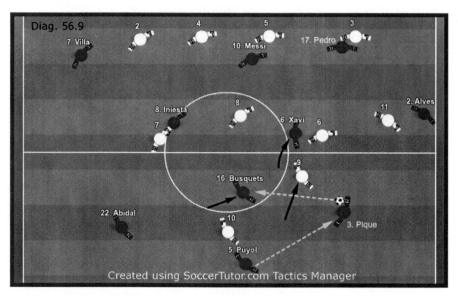

In a situation similar to the previous one, Xavi moves forward.

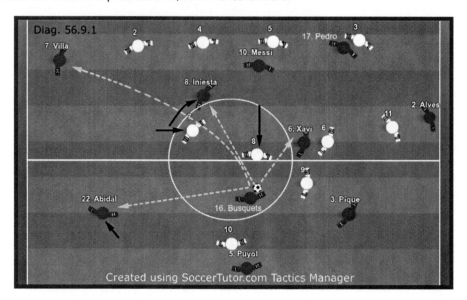

As Messi is too far away to provide support to Pique, the numerical superiority near the ball zone is provided by Busquets who shifts towards the ball carrier and receives.

ASSESSMENT

Busquets was the spare player in the central zone most often.

MOVEMENT INTO SPACE

On diagrams 56.10 and 56.10.1 the build up starts with Puyol who is positioned centrally.

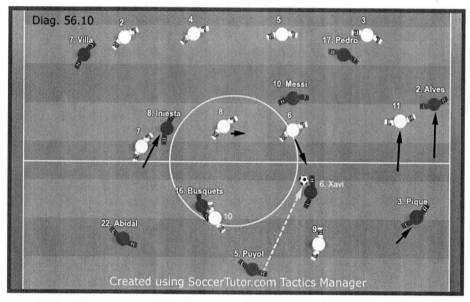

The first pass is directed to Xavi who receives.

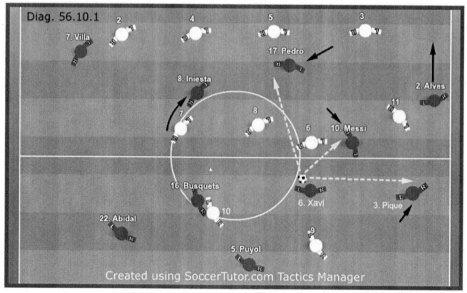

Considering where the opposition players are positioned, Barcelona's players move into areas of space to provide support to the new ball carrier.

☒ ASSESSMENT

A rhombus shape is created with Xavi, Messi, Iniesta and Pedro.

Pique is the spare player who provides another passing option and security.

RHOMBUS/DIAMOND SHAPE IN THE CENTRAL ZONE

On diagram 56.11 the ball is passed to Busquets, as Xavi is marked tightly.

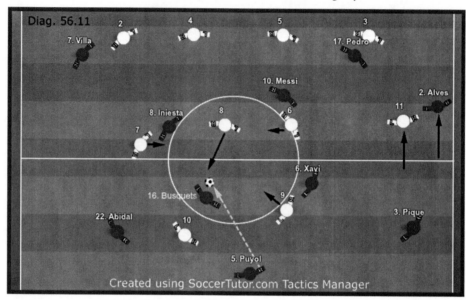

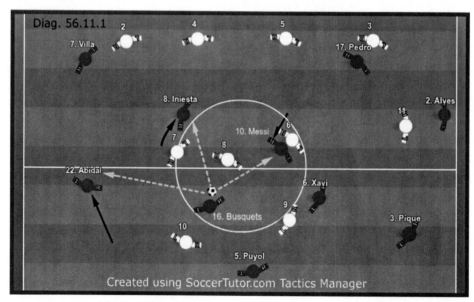

Busquets receives the ball half turned and has the passing options of Abidal, Iniesta and Messi (Diag.56.11.1).

 ASSESSMENT

Busquets' body shape is key to make sure that when he receives the ball he has all 3 passing options available to him.

FORWARD DROPPING DEEP TO MAINTAIN POSSESSION

Diagrams 56.12 and 56.12.1.

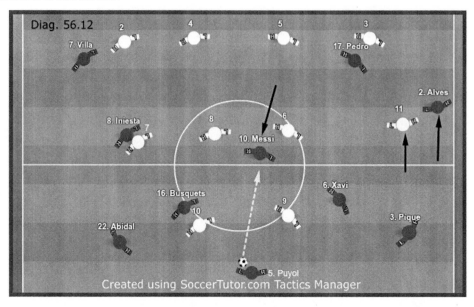

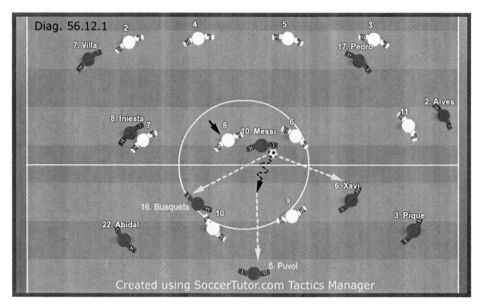

As the passing options to Xavi and Busquets are blocked off, Messi moves back in order to receive and pass the ball to one of them.

ASSESSMENT

Messi realises the team need to have a numerical superiority in the central zone, so drops back to help create one.

He simply passes the ball back to maintain possession for his team.

MOVEMENT: CREATING SPACE FOR OTHERS

Diagrams 56.13 and 56.13.1.

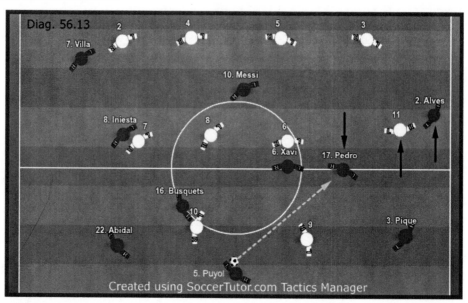

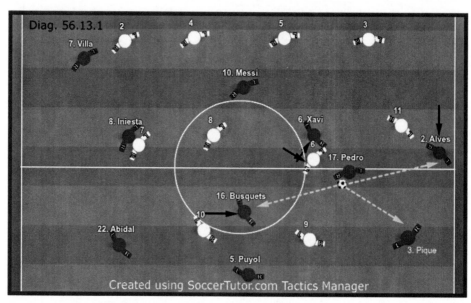

Pedro takes advantage of the free space created by Alves, who then moves back to receive and becomes one of the three available passing options.

EXAMPLE 2

Diagrams 56.14 and 56.14.1.

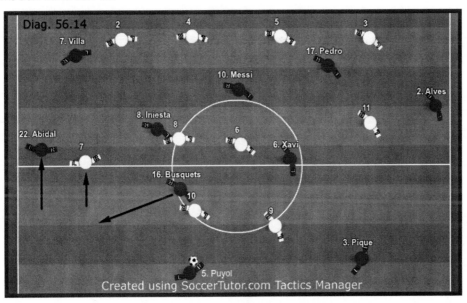

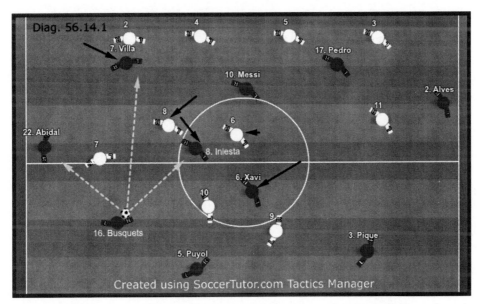

Abidal moves forward and creates space for Busquets who takes advantage of this and receives a pass from Puyol.

 ASSESSMENT

In both examples the advanced positions of the full backs occupy an opposition midfielder, who has to track them.

This creates space for a teammate to receive the ball unmarked.

USING THE CORRECT BODY SHAPE

Diagrams 56.15 and 56.15.1.

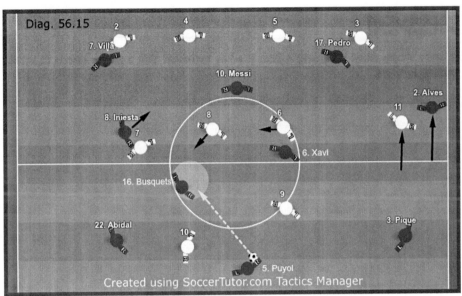

In a similar situation to diagram 56.11 the ball is directed to Busquets who has the proper body shape to receive and play the ball forward.

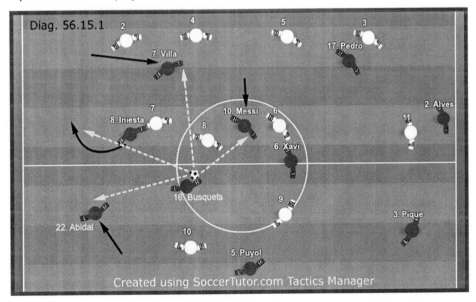

With this correct body shape Busquets can think quickly and pass the ball towards the players who are in supporting positions ahead, as well as towards Abidal who moves forward.

 ASSESSMENT

The correct body shape when receiving a pass is a key technical skill a player needs to maximise his available passing options.

MAINTAINING POSSESSION FROM WIDE POSITIONS

Diagrams 56.16 Abidal receives from Puyol.

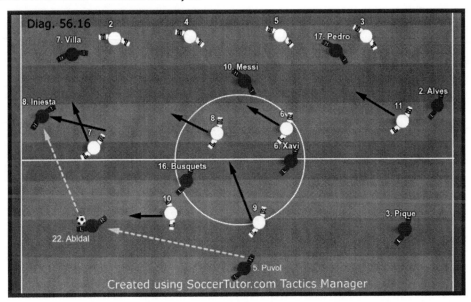

The ball is directed to Iniesta who opens up his body in his position near the sideline.

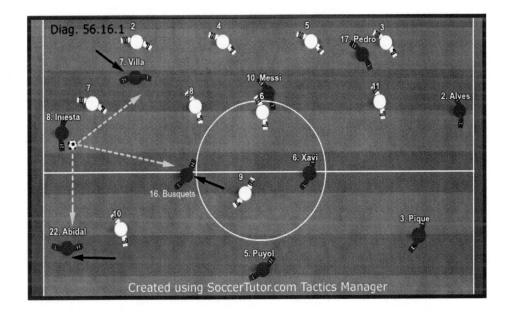

Because of the quick movement of the white team towards the ball zone and the No.7 putting pressure on Iniesta, Barcelona are unable to reach the third stage.

The focus turns to the retaining possession of the ball. (Diag 56.16.1)

 ASSESSMENT

When Barcelona did not have a numerical advantage around the ball zone they would simply seek to maintain possession.

DECISION MAKING IN THE FINAL THIRD

Diagrams 56.17 and 56.17.1.

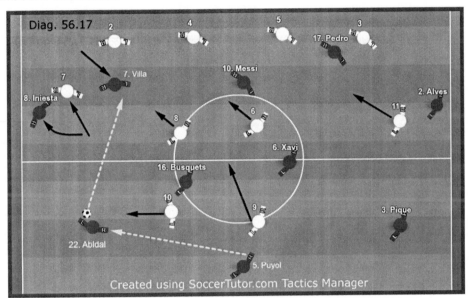

Abidal chooses to pass the ball to Villa, evading the midfield.

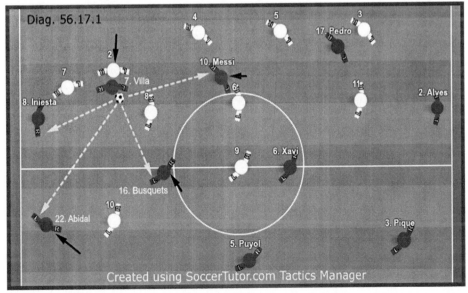

All the available options for the new ball carrier lead to the retaining of the ball, except for the pass towards Messi which leads to the final stage.

ASSESSMENT

The decision whether to try and enter the final stage of the attack was the decision of the player receiving a pass in the opposition half.

It was up to this player's judgment of the situation and to assess the other players' positioning.

EXAMPLE 2

Diagrams 56.18 and 56.18.1.

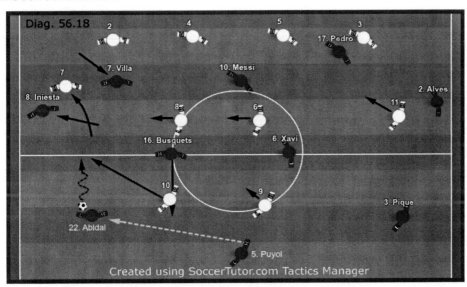

Abidal moves forward with the ball, while Busquets drops back to receive.

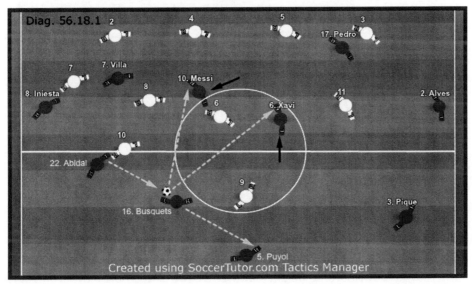

Busquets' pass to Messi can lead the team to the third stage depending on Messi's response to the situation.

The possible pass towards Xavi can definitely lead to the final stage of the attacking phase.

NUMERICAL DISADVANTAGE IN THE FINAL THIRD

Diagrams 56.19 and 56.19.1.

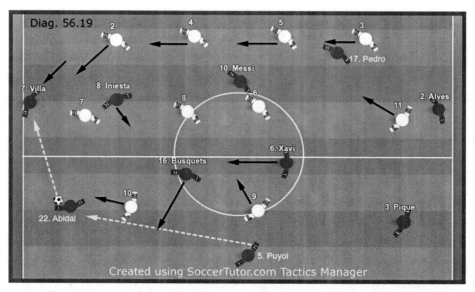

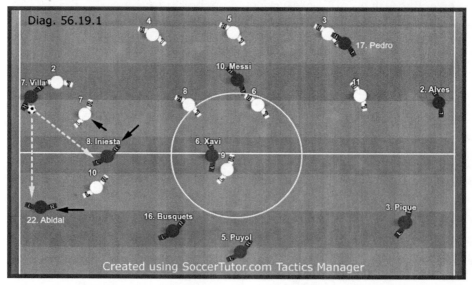

The movements of Villa and Iniesta are different. However, the two players both move in order to provide the appropriate support to the ball carrier. The ball is directed to Villa who receives with his back to the opponent's goal and he can only play to retain the ball possession.

The same tactical situation is shown on diagrams 56.20 and 56.20.1.

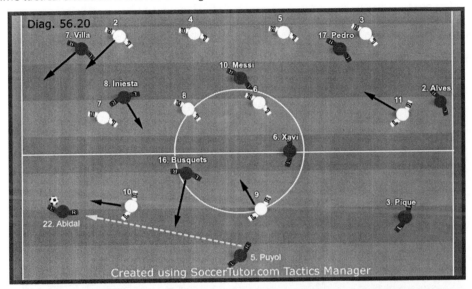

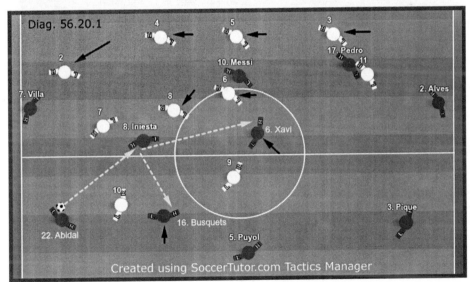

NUMERICAL SUPERIORITY

We see a different scenario on diagrams 56.21, 56.21.1, 56.22 and 56.22.1.

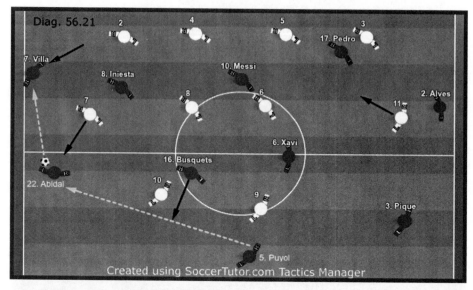

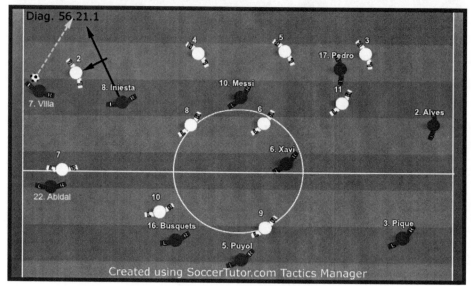

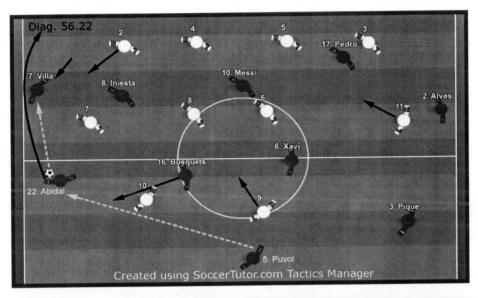

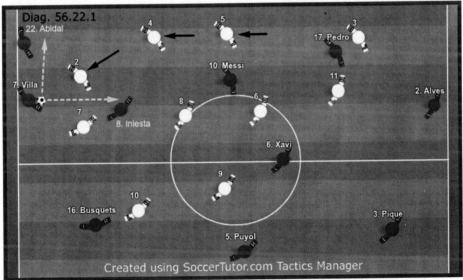

Barcelona create a numerical superiority around the ball zone in all of these situations and all the available passing options can lead to the final stage.

 ASSESSMENT

All these scenarios show the fluid triangle shape which maximises the passing options and creates 2v1 situations.

When the white No.7 moves forward and marks Abidal (Diag 56.21 & 56.21.1) Iniesta is able to exploit the space left on the flank to create a 2v1 situation against the right back. This then leads to the final stage of attack.

When the white No.7 chooses to mark Iniesta (Diag 56.22 & 56.22.1) the 2v1 is created when Abidal makes an overlapping run.

When the opposition used two forwards Busquets would would fill in to become one of three defenders.

his meant that a forward run from the full backs could create a 5v3 advantage in the midfield which meant Barca could get to the third stage much more easily.

CHAPTER 6
THE FIRST STAGE OF THE ATTACKING PHASE AGAINST THE 4-2-3-1 FORMATION

• Attacking down the flank..87
• Switching play 90
• Receiving with the correct body shape 92
• Exploiting Space...93
• Creating 3 Passing Options 94
• Receiving with your back to goal 96
• Body shape determining the next pass 97
• Approaching the third stage of attack..99
• Central midfield passing options 101
• Maintaining balance in the central zone 103
• Numerical superiority around the ball zone 105
• Wide Forwards 107
• Messi dropping deep 109
• Xavi's options from his central position 111

THE FIRST STAGE OF THE ATTACKING PHASE AGAINST THE 4-2-3-1 FORMATION

There were games where Barcelona used the formation shown on diagram 55.2, with only two players staying at the back.

By using this formation the team was more balanced during the attacking phase and could pursue any attacking actions from both sides.

The two full backs had more freedom to move forward.

Messi's position close to the midfield provided superiority in numbers and increased the available options for the ball carrier when the build up took place in the centre of the pitch.

When the opposition got even more compact in the central zone attempting to prevent the diagonal and vertical passes, there was plenty of free space down the flanks for Barcelona to create 2v1 situations.

On diagrams 57.1 up to 57.11, the way Barcelona developed the first stage of the attacking phase is presented for when the team had to face an opponent who used the 4-2-3-1 formation.

ATTACKING DOWN THE FLANK

Diagrams 57.1 and 57.1.1.

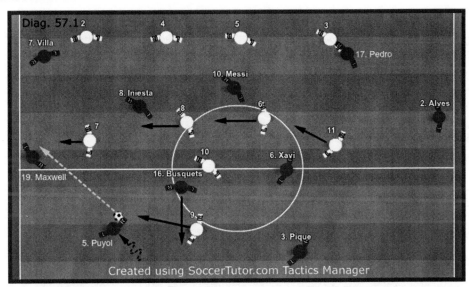

Puyol moves forward with the ball. Busquets drops in and covers his position.

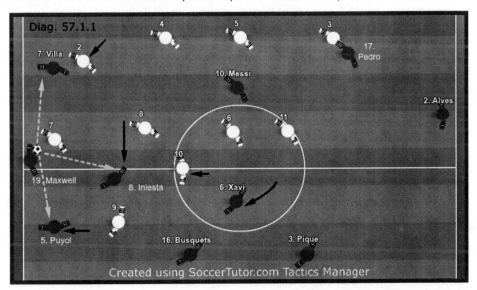

The pass is directed to Maxwell and Villa together with Iniesta give support to him. As there is equality in numbers on the flank, (2v2 situation), the build up goes on in order to retain possession of the ball.

EXAMPLE 2

Diagrams 57.2 and 57.2.1.

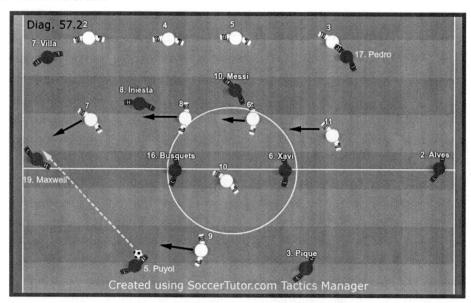

Puyol does not move up this time, but passes immediately to Maxwell.

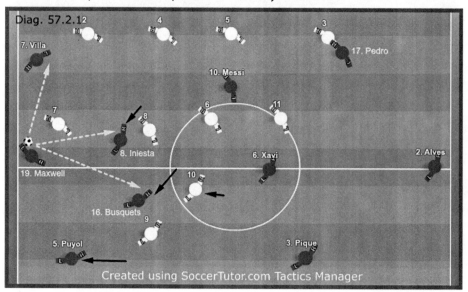

As Busquets takes up a supporting position deep in the centre of the field, Iniesta does not have to move back to receive.

ASSESSMENT

The players shift over from central positions to provide support to the player in possession on the flank.

SWITCHING PLAY

On diagram 57.3, the first pass is directed to Iniesta.

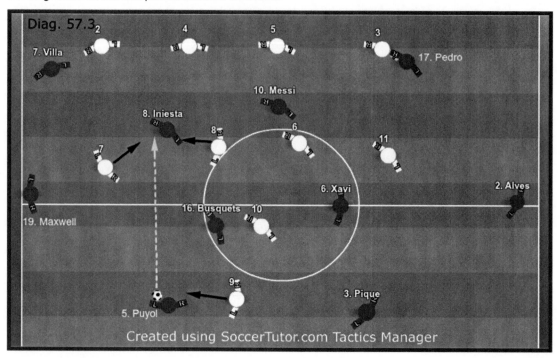

If the new ball carrier (Iniesta) manages to turn towards the opponent's goal, there will be many possibilities for Barcelona to reach the final stage.

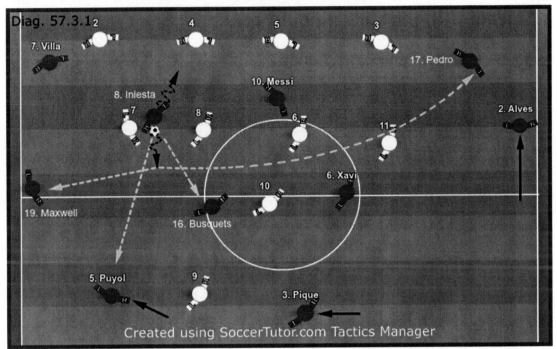

Diag. 57.3.1₂

7. Villa
4
5
3
17. Pedro
8. Iniesta
10. Messi
2. Alves
7
8
6
11
6. Xavi
10
19. Maxwell
16. Busquets
5. Puyol
9
3. Pique

Created using SoccerTutor.com Tactics Manager

If turning is too difficult to achieve and Iniesta is forced to play with his back towards the opposition's goal he has many other options.

Iniesta can pass back to Busquets or Puyol or receive, move back with the ball and switch play towards Maxwell or Pedro (diagram 57.3.1).

The changing of the point of attack with the long ball towards Pedro was a very common passing option when Barcelona used this formation.

 ## ASSESSMENT

When the opposition were able to make the area around the ball compact Barca always had an outlet on the flank.

RECEIVING WITH THE CORRECT BODY SHAPE

On diagrams 57.4 and 57.4.1, the ball is passed to Busquets.

If Busquets has the proper body stance (with his face towards the opposition's goal) when receiving, he will be able to pass the ball forward to the available options.

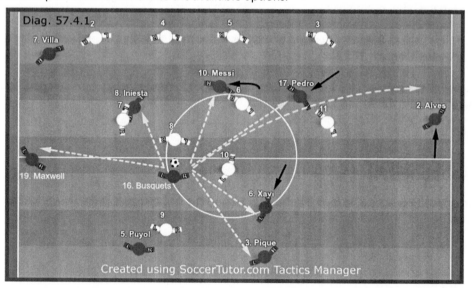

If Busquets receives with his face towards his own goal and is being put under the opponent's pressure, the only available options for him are the passes to Xavi or Pique which only help the team to retain ball possession.

EXPLOITING SPACE

Diagrams 57.5 and 57.5.1.

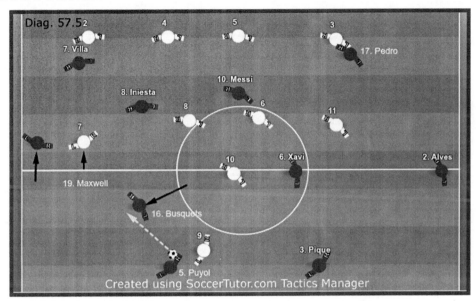

Busquets takes advantage of the free space created by Maxwell's forward run.

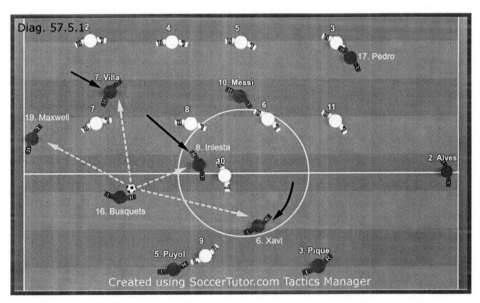

Maxwell, Villa and Iniesta are the available passing options, while Xavi takes up a position which will lead to a possible change of the point of attack if the pass is directed to him.

CREATING 3 PASSING OPTIONS

Diagrams 57.6 and 57.6.1.

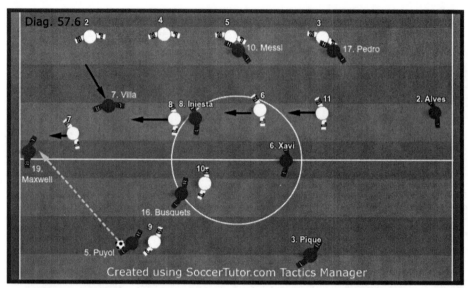

Iniesta's positioning near the centre and away from the ball zone leads Villa to move to the top of the rhombus/diamond (Maxwell, Villa, Busquets and Puyol), in order to provide one extra passing option for Puyol.

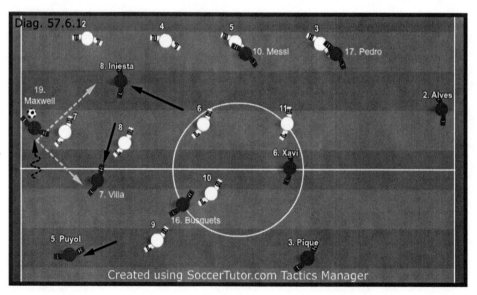

The pass from Puyol to Maxwell makes Villa drop back and Iniesta move diagonally, both for the purpose of providing support.

ASSESSMENT

Villa's movement here, which takes the white No.8 with him, provides space for Iniesta to be in an advanced position free of marking.

RECEIVING WITH YOUR BACK TO GOAL

Diagrams 57.7 and 57.7.1.

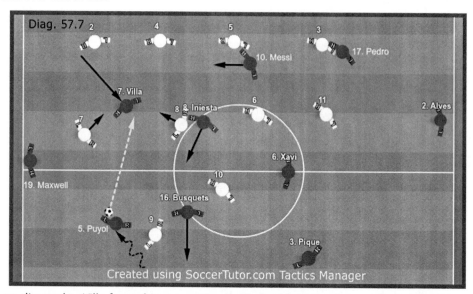

The pass directed to Villa forces him to receive the ball with his back turned towards the opponent's goal.

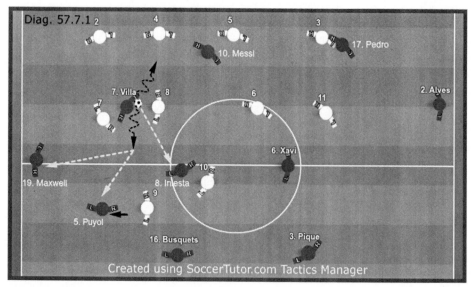

This means that Villa has to choose between a direct back pass to Iniesta or to receive and move with the ball and then pass to Maxwell or Puyol. If there is a possibility to turn towards the opposition's goal, it is very likely for the team to reach the final stage.

BODY SHAPE DETERMINING THE NEXT PASS

On diagram 57.8 Puyol passes to Iniesta who makes a movement to receive.

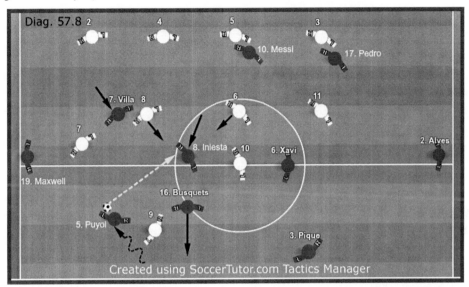

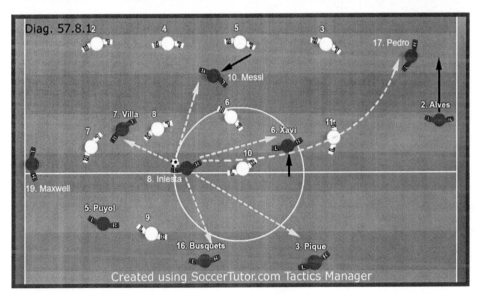

The body shape of Iniesta determines if the ball is passed forward or backward (Diag.57.8.1).

ASSESSMENT

Body shape is key again there o determine how many options the player in possession will have and whether the pass will be forward or back.

There was often many passing options available which would include:

• Short passes
• Passes backwards to change the point of attack
• Long passes to switch play immediately

APPROACHING THE THIRD STAGE OF ATTACK

On diagrams 57.9 and 57.9.1, Pique passes the ball to Busquets.

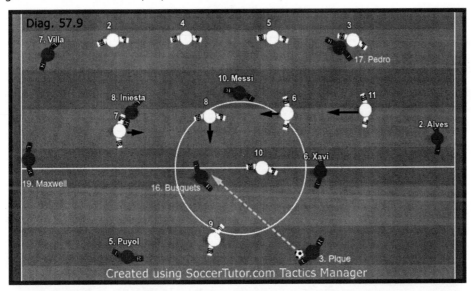

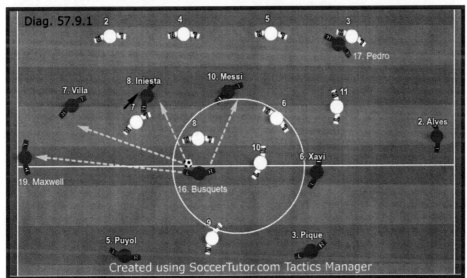

The available passing options given by the supporting players can all lead to the third stage.

The pass towards Villa or Maxwell can lead to a 2v1 situation in favour of Barcelona and the pass towards Messi or Iniesta, who move into the space between the opposition's midfield and defensive line, can lead to a final vertical or diagonal pass.

 ASSESSMENT

The Barcelona players demonstrate great positioning here.

Four players are unmarked and are able to take their team to the third stage if they receive a pass.

CENTRAL MIDFIELD PASSING OPTIONS

On diagrams 57.10 and 57.10.1 Xavi has dropped back to receive the ball.

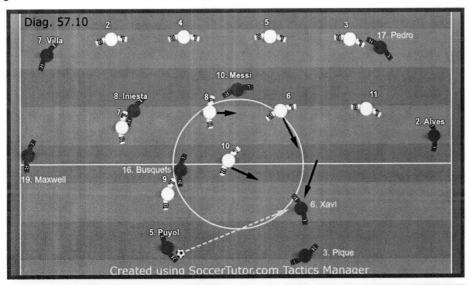

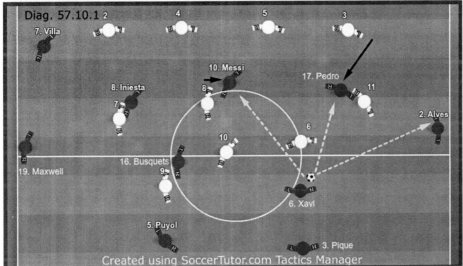

As soon as Xavi becomes the new ball carrier, Pedro and Messi move to give support.

 ASSESSMENT

Pedro's movement inside provides space for Alves to be free of marking on the right flank.

EXAMPLE 2

Diagrams 57.11 and 57.11.1

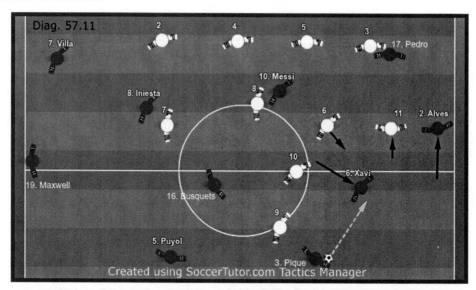

In a similar situation to the previous one, Xavi takes advantage of the free space and receives the ball.

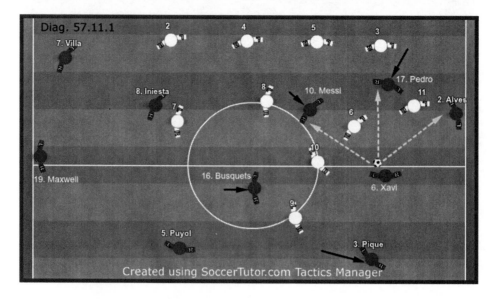

Pedro moves in the same way, while Messi (because of No.6's positioning), moves deep to give support.

MAINTAINING BALANCE IN THE CENTRAL ZONE

Diagrams 57.12 and 57.12.1.

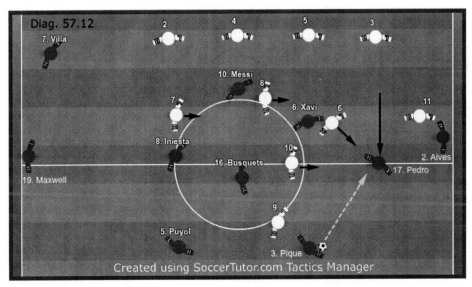

Pedro receives the first pass, while Xavi takes up a position away from the ball zone.

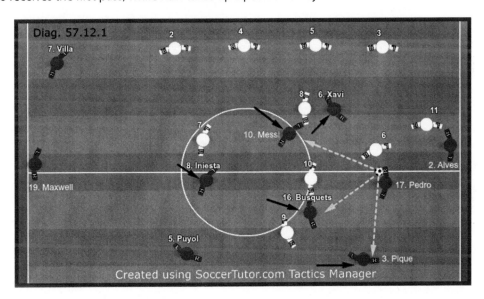

Busquets moves towards the ball carrier to give support and to provide balance because of Xavi's movement higher up the pitch.

Messi moves deep in order to give support and help create superiority in numbers near the ball zone.

Xavi moves forward to retain the balance of the formation.

 ## ASSESSMENT

The team's fluidity and cohesion is demonstrated again here, as all the players in the team are capable of covering the others' position.

NUMERICAL SUPERIORITY AROUND THE BALL ZONE

Diagram 57.13 shows Barca passing along the back line (Pique to Alves).

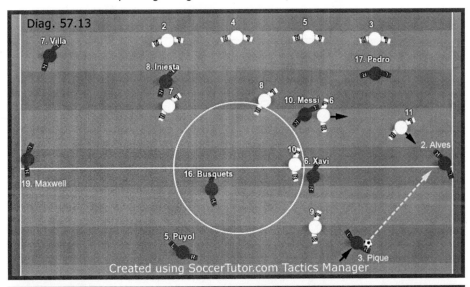

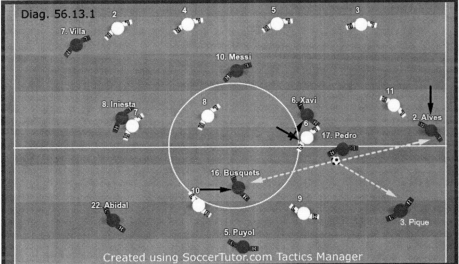

Here the creation of superiority in numbers down the flank is not possible as there is a 2v2 situation.

The players focus on retaining the possession of the ball by outnumbering the opposition near the ball zone.

That is why Pedro drops back, while Xavi and Pique move to give support to the ball carrier.

ASSESSMENT

The rhombus/diamond shape provides options so Barca can maintain possession.

WIDE FORWARDS

Diagrams 57.14 and 57.14.1.

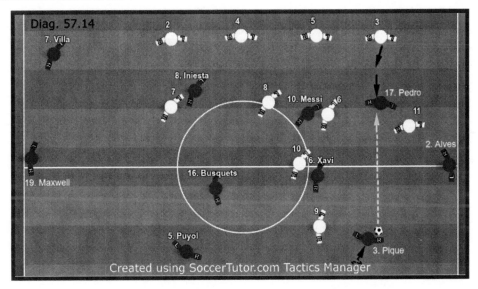

After receiving, Pedro has two available backwards passing options (Xavi and Alves) which would help the team to retain the ball and one pass towards Messi, which can lead to the third stage.

 ASSESSMENT

The decision of whether to simply maintain possession or attempt to enter the final stage was often made by the wide forwards.

This movement inside and off the flank was typical for both wide forwards.

This created space for the two full backs to make advancing runs.

MESSI DROPPING DEEP

On diagram 57.15 Xavi can not receive the ball because of No.9's positioning.

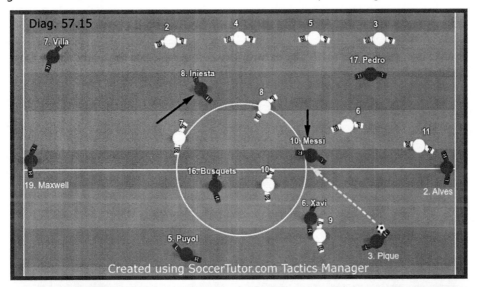

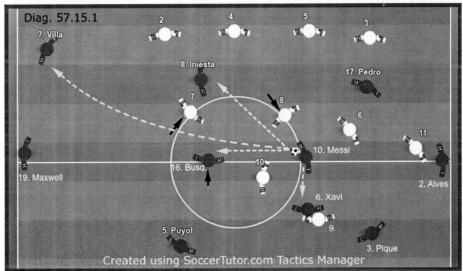

As Messi moves back to use the free space, Iniesta pushes up in order to provide balance (Diag 57.15.1).

When Messi becomes the new ball carrier his available passing options are Iniesta, Xavi and Villa.

The last passing option to Villa, with the contribution of Maxwell, can lead to superiority in numbers on the left.

 ASSESSMENT

Messi would often join the midfield to create superiority in numbers.

This helped Barca make successful passes but could leave them without a centre forward.

One of the midfielders would counter this by moving forwards to maintain the teams' shape. On diagram 57.15 Iniesta does this.

XAVI'S OPTIONS FROM HIS CENTRAL POSITION

Finally we have diagrams 57.16 and 57.16.1.

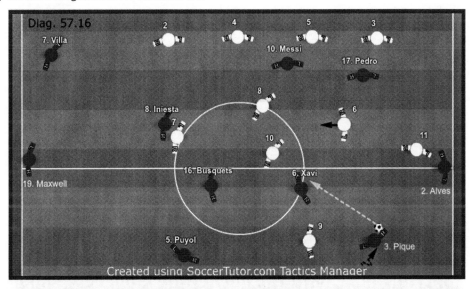

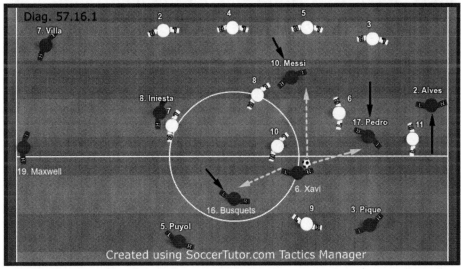

Xavi, after receiving, can pass to Messi, Pedro or Busquets.

 ASSESSMENT

The forwards again drop deeper to create short passing options for the ball carrier .

CHAPTER 7
HOW BARCELONA DEAL WITH THE OPPOSITION'S PRESSING DURING THE FIRST STAGE OF THE ATTACKING PHASE

• **Vertical passes against the 4-4-2** 115
• **Advancing full backs creating space**...116
• **Passing out from the goalkeeper** 117

HOW BARCELONA DEAL WITH THE OPPOSITION'S PRESSING DURING THE FIRST STAGE OF THE ATTACKING PHASE

As already mentioned, during the first stage Barcelona wanted to move the ball from the defenders to the midfielders, or to the forwards who dropped deep by using mainly short passing.

Even when under severe pressure from the opposition, the main aim of the team was to break down the pressing by using a short passing game.

A strong point of the team was its ability to find a way to move the ball to the spare player which the team usually had in midfield or on the flanks. However, in cases where there were not any available short passing options, the team used long passes towards particular parts of the field.

In this chapter tactical situations will be shown where Barcelona had to overcome the opposition pressing close to their penalty area.

The positions of Barcelona's players were taken up in relation to the formation the team used during the attacking phase with either a two or three man defence.

In the two man defence and with Valdes being in control of the ball, the two central defenders move nearer the sidelines, the two full backs moved forward, while the defensive midfielder drops into a deep position.

This last action by Busquets, together with Messi's movement deeper created a numerical superiority in the central zone for Barcelona. The opposing team usually found this very difficult to cope with (diagram 58.1).

Diag. 58.2

When the team used a three man defence, the defensive midfielder did not have to drop deep.

Messi's frequent positioning in midfield again helped outnumber the opposition (diagram 58.2).

With Villa and Pedro staying in wide positions the opposition were prevented from pushing their full backs forward. The teams that attempted to apply pressure without having one of their central defenders push up to follow Messi in midfield struggled. They could not deal with Barcelona's build up play effectively.

Whenever the opposition had a central defender closely marking Lionel Messi as he dropped into midfield it obviously left a gap in the centre of the defence. This would create problems if the application of pressing was not successful.

On the diagrams to follow, Barcelona are under pressure from a team using the 4-4-2 formation.

When the opposition used the 4-2-3-1 formation, the attacking midfielder took over the role of the second forward and there were not many differences from the situations which are analysed below.

VERTICAL PASSES AGAINST THE 4-4-2

Diagrams 59.1 and 59.1.1.

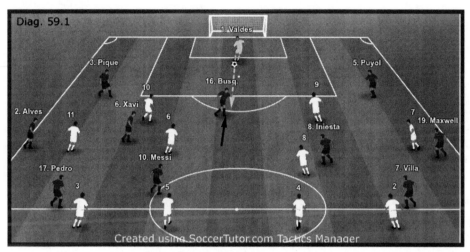

Diag. 59.1

Busquets drops deep in order to outnumber the opposition outside Barcelona's box and receives the ball unmarked.

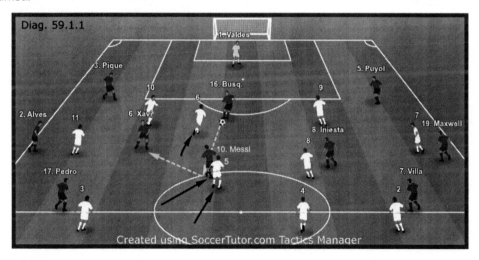

Diag. 59.1.1

As No.6 tries to put pressure on him, the ball is moved via Messi to Xavi who is the free player in midfield.

 **ASSESSMENT**

White No.5 has to close down the ball, so leaves Xavi unmarked to receive the ball in space.

ADVANCING FULL BACKS CREATING SPACE

Diagrams 59.2 and 59.2.1.

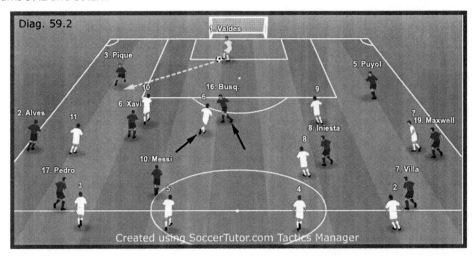

Busquets drops deep and is under No.6's close marking. This means that in midfield there is a situation of 2v1 in favour of Barcelona (Alves and Xavi v white No. 11) without Messi having to drop back.

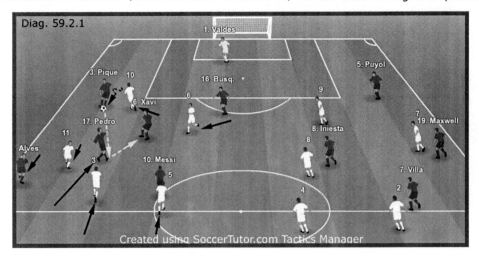

The ball is moved through Pique and Pedro to Xavi, who is the free man in midfield.

 ASSESSMENT

Barcelona almost always used short passes to build up play. Alves creates the space here with his movement.

PASSING OUT FROM THE GOALKEEPER

On diagram 59.3 the white team puts pressure on Valdes.

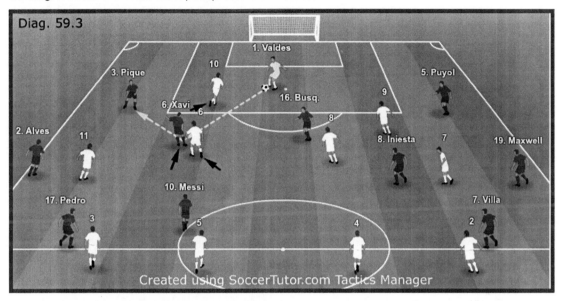

Diag. 59.3

Created using SoccerTutor.com Tactics Manager

No.10's movement leaves Pique free of marking.

The ball reaches Pique through Xavi.

 ASSESSMENT

Valdes has good technique on the ball and with his passing.

He is a vital part of Barca playing out from the back.

EXAMPLE 2

On diagram 59.4, Pique receives and moves forward.

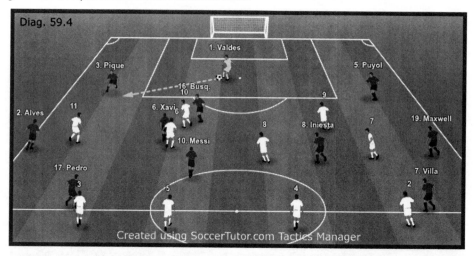

No.11 makes a move to press him and leaves Alves free of marking. The ball is moved from Pique to Alves through Pedro.

 ASSESSMENT

With Busquets' deep position Barca outnumbered the forwards 3v2 near to the penalty area and in this case the oppositions' wide player (No.11) has had to push forward, leaving Alves unmarked.

EXAMPLE 3

Diagrams 59.5 and 59.5.1.

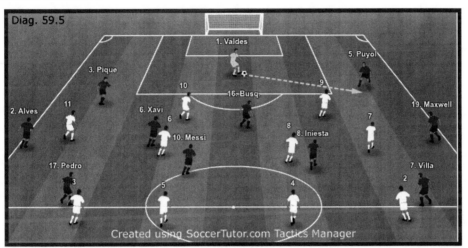

Messi's positioning in midfield forces the midfielders of the opposition to leave Busquets free of marking. No.9 and No.10 of the white team take up positions which enable them to mark all three Barcelona players (Puyol, Busquets and Pique) around the penalty area.

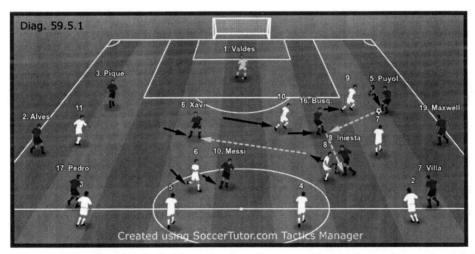

The first pass is directed to Puyol, who then passes to Busquets. No.10 tries to change the 4v2 situation in midfield by making a move to mark Busquets.

As No.6 moves back to mark Messi, Xavi becomes the free player in midfield.

The pass is aimed towards Xavi after Iniesta's control and movement with the ball.

 ASSESSMENT

Messi joining the midfield again allows Barca to have a player free of marking in the centre of the field (Xavi, diag 59.5.1).

EXAMPLE 4

On diagram 59.6 Puyol receives the first pass and moves forward.

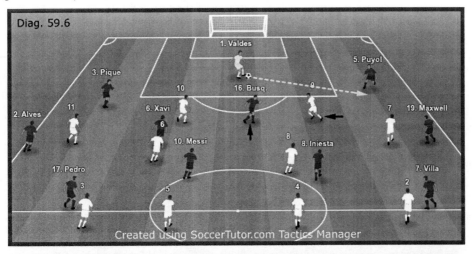

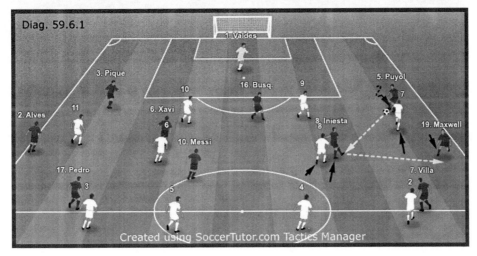

No.7 moves to contest the ball carrier. The ball is moved to Maxwell via Iniesta (Diag. 59.6.1).

✐ ASSESSMENT

With Barca outnumbering the opposition 3v2 near to the penalty area the oppositions' wide player (No.7) has had to push forward, leaving Maxwell unmarked.

EXAMPLE 5

On diagrams 59.7 and 59.8, the opposition are pressing high up the pitch and this forces Valdes to make a long pass towards the flanks, where Barcelona outnumber their opponents.

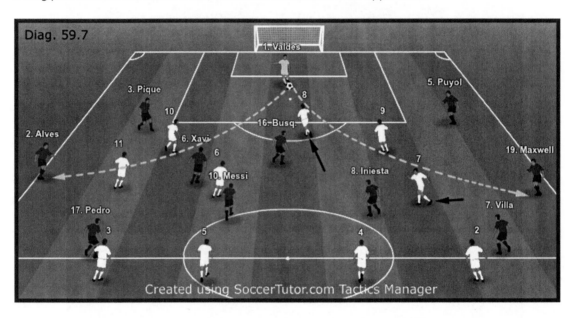

Specifically on diagram 59.7, No.7 moves towards the centre in order to block off a possible pass to Iniesta.

When the pressure on Valdes is being applied through the centre, he makes a long pass towards the sidelines.

There was usually a free Barcelona player or numerical superiority in favour of Barca in that area.

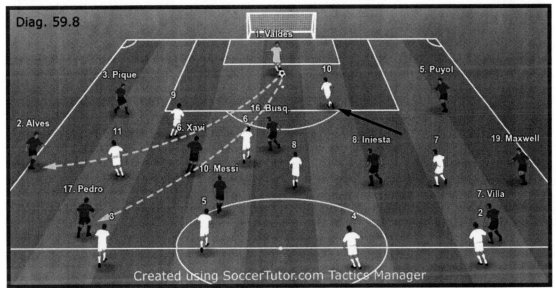

Diag. 59.8

Created using SoccerTutor.com Tactics Manager

On diagram 59.8, as the pressure is being applied from the left side of Barca, the pass is made towards the opposite direction, targeting the wide forward (Pedro) or the right back (Alves).

 ## ASSESSMENT

When the opposition attempted to create a 3v3 situation near to Barcelona's penalty area they were left vulnerable in midfield where it became 5v3 in Barcelona's favour..

EXAMPLE 6

On diagrams 60.1 and 60.1.1, the team used the formation from diagram 58.2 with three defenders (Pique, Puyol and Abidal).

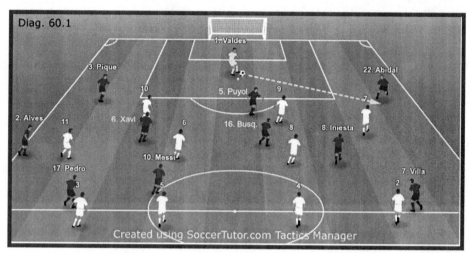

This formation forces No.7 to move up in order to put pressure on Abidal as soon as he becomes the ball carrier. The positioning of No.8 is such that it enables him to mark both Iniesta and Busquets.

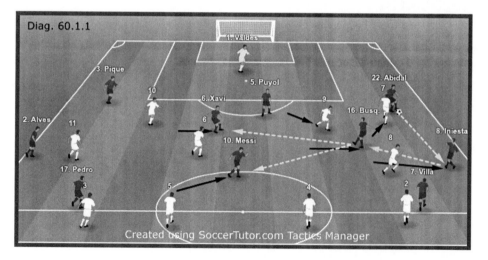

When the ball is passed to Abidal and Iniesta moves towards the sideline to receive, No.8 is unable to put immediate pressure on him. Iniesta has enough time on the ball to pass to Busquets who then has the options of passing to Messi or Xavi.

EXAMPLE 7

Diagrams 60.2 and 60.3.

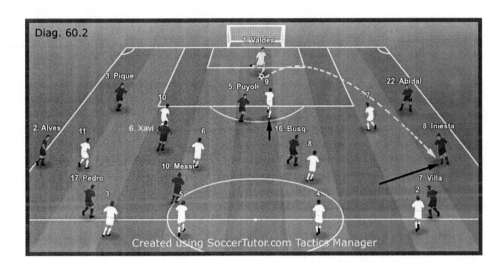

The long pass is directed to Iniesta who moves near the sideline free of marking.

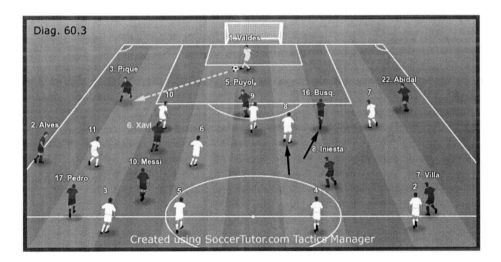

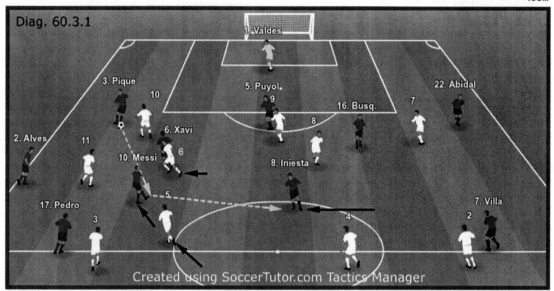

Diag. 60.3.1

On diagrams 60.3 and 60.3.1, No.8's movement to follow Busquets leaves Iniesta unmarked, who after Messi's pass, receives the ball completely free of marking in the centre of the field.

 ## ASSESSMENT

Iniesta's movement prevents No.8 from being able to mark 2 players.

Barca were brilliant at constantly moving to prevent any opposition players being able to cover more than one player.

This meant that superiority in numbers was often achieved around the ball.

CHAPTER 8
BARCELONA DURING THE SECOND AND THIRD STAGE OF THE ATTACKING PHASE ON THE RIGHT SIDE

• **Build up play using a three man defence** 129
• **Messi's wide movement** 131
• **Diagonal runs in the final third** 132
• **Attacking down the flank** 134
• **Attacking down the flank: Overlapping runs**...135
• **Combination play near the penalty area**..136
• **2 v 2 Attacking down the flank**...137
• **2 v 1 Attacking down the flank**...143
• **Decision making and maintaining possession** 144
• **Messi's driving runs from deep** 145
• **Messi maintaining possession** 146
• **Messi playing from the right flank** 147

THE BUILD UP PLAY USING A TWO MAN DEFENCE

• **Formations**..150
• **Daniel Alves's passing options** 153
• **Messi's movement into 'the hole'** 154
• **Iniesta advancing into Messi's position** 156
• **Advancing runs from the left back**..158
• **Messi in the central zone** 160
• **Switching play** 162

BARCELONA DURING THE SECOND AND THIRD STAGE OF THE ATTACKING PHASE ON THE RIGHT SIDE

If someone watches Barcelona play during the attacking phase, they will notice the lack of set patterns.

The Barcelona players have great patience and ability to analyse the tactical situations quickly in order to find the opposition's weak point. Only once this weak point is found, will the players move to the third stage of the attacking phase.

Except for when they enter the final stage the team does not risk losing possession. The players move almost everywhere on the field trying to create the ideal formations needed for an effective passing game.

The fact that the players have the freedom to move and switch positions during the attacking phase does not mean that they are undisciplined or that they build up play without a plan.

The players seem to make movements that unbalance the team at some points. However these movements are followed by others, which seek to restore the lost balance immediately.

Nevertheless, the two basic formations used during the attacking phase that were analysed in a previous chapter provide different ways of building up play depending on the tactical context.

In order for the analysis of the second and third stage to be as simple as possible, the field is divided into two parts. The build up play has been separated into build up from the right side and build up from the left side.

When the team used the three man defence, the differences in the movements and the combinations that took place on the right side were remarkable in relation to the ones on the left.

When the two man defence was used, the movements of the players and the combinations between them were similar on both sides.

BUILD UP PLAY USING A THREE MAN DEFENCE

During the build up using the three man defence, Messi drops back towards the right causing an overload on this side.

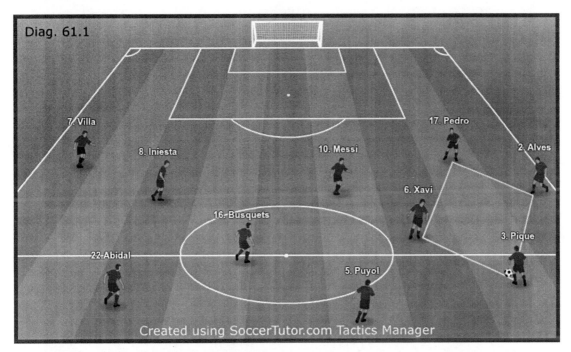

Diag. 61.1

The numerical superiority in favour of Barcelona on the right side resulted in a higher percentage of possession on this side compared to the left one.

The build up play on the right depended on the effective passing game in limited spaces and the mobility of the players, who switched positions regularly.

The build up play from the left, because of the presence of only three players (Villa, Iniesta/Keita, Abidal/Maxwell) on this side, was more fluid and depended on attacking the available free space.

Specifically, Barcelona's build up play on the right was based on the rhombus/diamond shape created by the positioning of Pique, Alves, Pedro and Xavi (with Pique being its base).

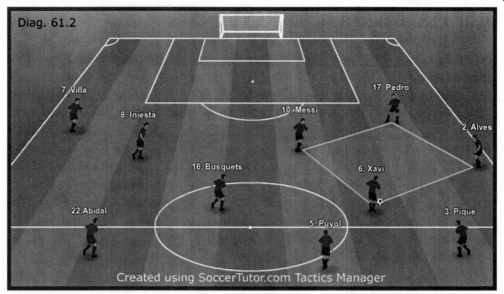

This rhombus/diamond here is created by the positioning of Alves, Pedro. Messi and Xavi at its base (diag. 61.2).

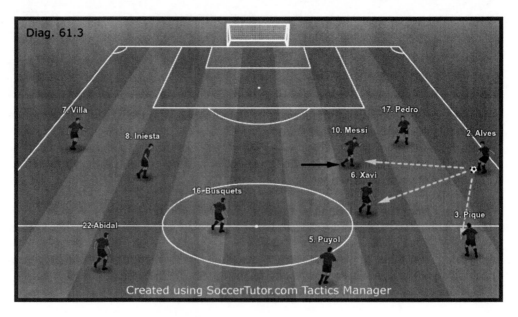

When the right back was in possession of the ball, the switching of play could be carried out through the midfielders (Messi, Xavi), or the defenders (Pique) - (diag. 61.3).

The mobility of the players could result in the switching of positions without changing the shape of the team.

MESSI'S WIDE MOVEMENT

Diagrams 61.4 and 61.5.

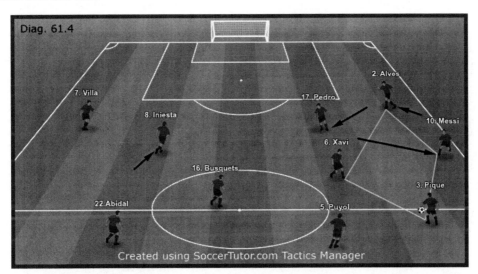

This diagram shows the new positions occupied by the players when Messi makes one of his typical movements towards the side line using the free space created by Alves' forward run.

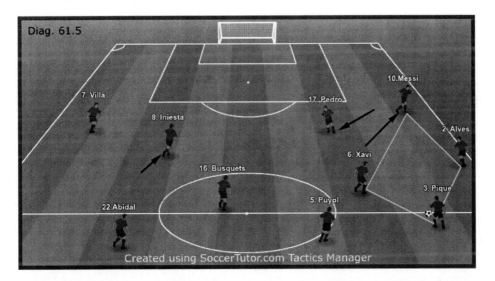

When Messi moved wide to receive the ball free of marking he would then make driving runs towards the centre. These runs usually ended in a shot on goal or a diagonal or vertical final pass towards the players who were breaking into the box. The possible receivers of these passes were Villa, Iniesta, Pedro and at times Xavi.

DIAGONAL RUNS IN THE FINAL THIRD

Villa and Iniesta were usually the players who took advantage of the final passes of Messi by moving diagonally. When Villa made the first move (diagonal run) towards the opposition's penalty area, Iniesta's starting position was a few metres behind him.

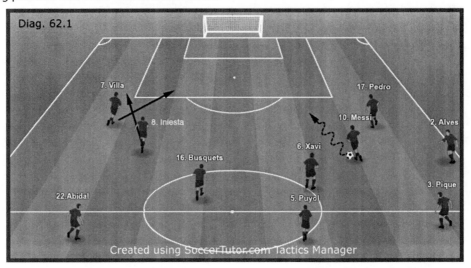

Villa was the one who broke into the box, while Iniesta took up a wider position (diag. 62.1).

In this case Iniesta was in a more advanced position and carried out the diagonal movement first. So this time he was the one who entered the penalty area and Villa provided the width with his run (diagram 62.2).

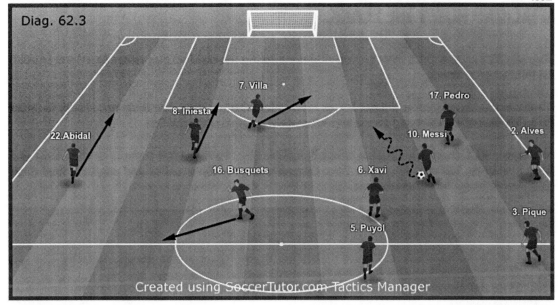

Diag. 62.3

If both of them moved diagonally towards the box, the attacking width was provided by the full back's forward run (diagram 62.3).

ASSESSMENT

As an attacking team Barca would strive to make runs into the penalty area, especially when Messi had the ball.

They would also create an option out wide to provide an outlet to switch the play.

ATTACKING DOWN THE FLANK

Diagrams 63.1 up to 63.13.3 show tactical situations during the build up play where Barcelona entered the third stage of attack.

Whenever the circumstances did not favour moving into the last stage, the team would seek to retain the ball possession by carrying on the second stage or going back to the first.

On diagram 63.1, there is a situation where Barcelona create a numerical superiority with Alves and Pedro against No.3 of the white team. Barca take advantage of this situation and reach the final stage with a low cross by Pedro into the box.

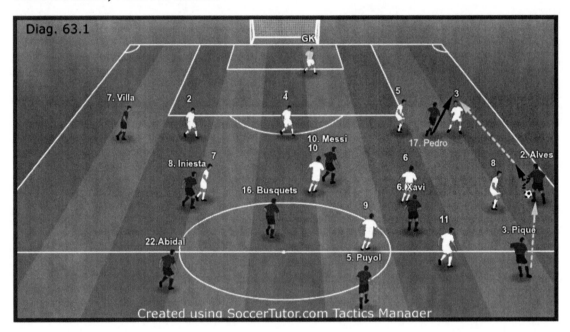

Pedro makes a run in behind No.3 to receive Alves' pass free in space. After receiving, he moves towards the box and crosses the ball into the penalty area.

ATTACKING DOWN THE FLANK: OVERLAPPING RUNS

Diagram 63.2.

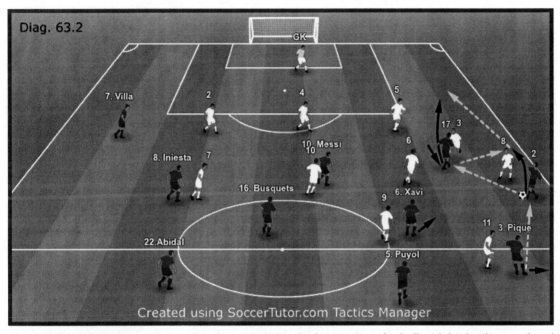

Alves works with Pedro to outnumber the opposition. Pedro receives the ball with his back to goal and his next pass helps Bara reach the last stage.

✎ ASSESSMENT

Alves' forward runs were a constant threat to the opposition, using his pace to reach the third stage of attack.

COMBINATION PLAY NEAR THE PENALTY AREA

On diagram 63.3, a situation develops near the white team's penalty area.

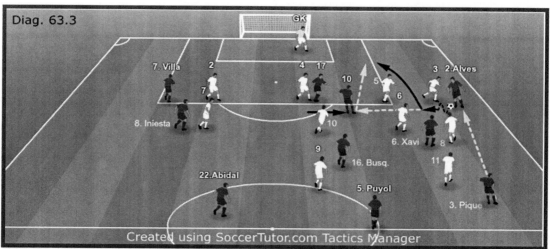

Alves becomes the ball carrier and as he does not have the chance to make the cross, he moves towards the centre. Messi gives support and Alves goes for the one-two.

In a similar situation Messi passes back to Xavi who makes a long pass to Iniesta in order to change the point of attack (diag. 63.3.1).

 ## ASSESSMENT

Messi would often have the choice between a final pass into the penalty area or to a free player out wide.

2 V 2 ATTACKING DOWN THE FLANK

On diagram 63.4, there is a situation of 2v2 on the right flank.

Diag. 63.4

As there is no numerical advantage Alves does not seek to move on to the third stage, but focuses on retaining the ball.

Pedro drops back into the free space and receives, then switches the play through Puyol.

EXAMPLE 2

On diagram 63.5, there is another situation of 2v2 in the same part of the field.

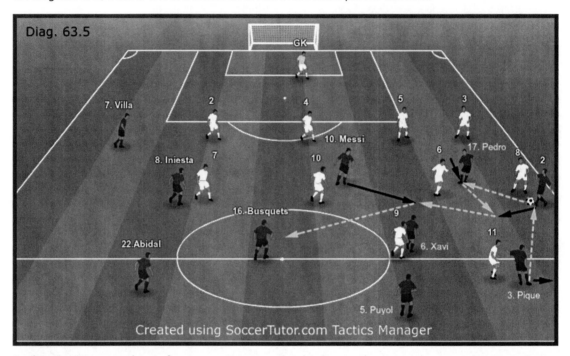

As the circumstances do not favour moving on to the third stage the team tries to retain possession.

Pedro drops back to receive and passes back to Alves, who gives support.

Using the correct body shape Alves seeks to change the point of attack through Messi.

 ## ASSESSMENT

When the situation was not right to advance to the third stage, many options would be available to pass back and change the point of attack.

EXAMPLE 3

On diagram 63.6, Pique's pass is directed to Pedro who moves back to receive.

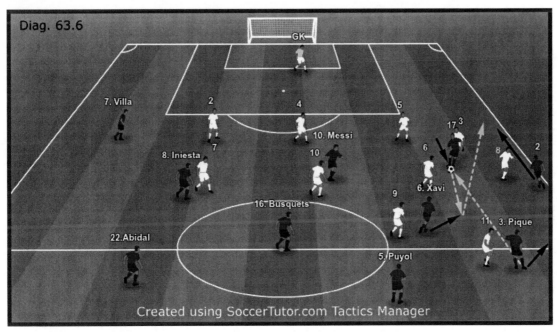

Diag. 63.6

His movement is being followed by No.3 who creates free space for Alves.

Barcelona take advantage of the opponent's weak point, as Alves attacks the free space and receives the diagonal pass from Xavi.

 ## ASSESSMENT

When the left back follows Pedro's movement, Alves is able to use his pace to exploit the space in behind.

EXAMPLE 4

On diagram 63.7, we have a similar situation to the previous one.

Diag. 63.7

7. Villa

10. Messi

8. Iniesta

6. Xavi

22.Abidal

16-Busquets

5. Puyol

3. Pique

2. Alves

GK

Created using SoccerTutor.com Tactics Manager

The same space is not available and the situation does not favour Barca entering the last stage.

Xavi, after receiving is being put under pressure, so passes back to Pique who moves forward.

Puyol gives support to him, while Busquets and Iniesta drop back to retain the team's balance.

 ASSESSMENT

Barca were very intelligent and only attempted to enter the third stage when there was a weakness in the opposition's defensive line.

EXAMPLE 5

Diagrams 63.8 and 63.8.1.

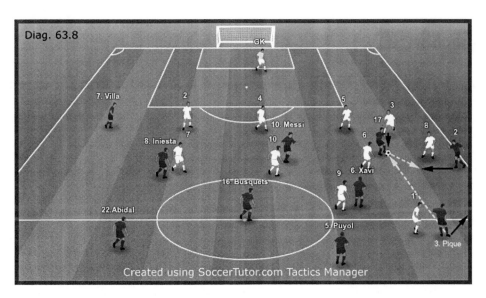

Pedro receives the ball and Alves moves to support him and finally receives Pedro's back pass.

Alves makes a driving run towards the centre through the gap in midfield and passes to Messi.

Considering Messi's ability at dribbling and making the final pass, four Barcelona players move in order to receive in behind the opposition's defensive line.

Messi also has the option of shooting at goal even when under pressure.

 # ASSESSMENT

Messi's superior ability allowed players to commit themselves to advanced positions as it was very likely the pass would be a good one.

2 V 1 ATTACKING DOWN THE FLANK

On diagram 63.9, Pique's pass is directed to Xavi.

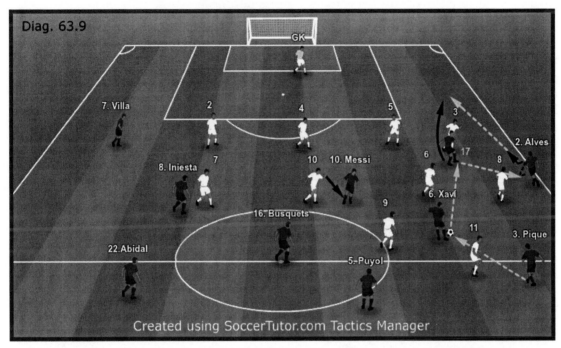

Diag. 63.9

Created using SoccerTutor.com Tactics Manager

Xavi passes the ball to Pedro, who combines with Alves taking advantage of No.8's poor position.

The 2v1 situation leads to Pedro receiving the ball behind the opposition's defensive line and delivering a low cross into the penalty area.

 ASSESSMENT

Alves' importance is again illustrated here.

If the left midfielder did not track the runs well enough a 2v1 situation would be created easily on the right flank.

DECISION MAKING AND MAINTAINING POSSESSION

On diagram 63.10, there is a situation similar to the previous one.

Diag. 63.10

Due to No.8's good positioning, Pedro passes to Alves and supports him to receive again.

Pedro once again becomes the ball carrier and contributes by retaining possession, as Xavi is being marked by No.9.

Puyol moves across to provide another option as the spare man.

MESSI'S DRIVING RUNS FROM DEEP

On diagram 63.11, Pique passes to Xavi and he passes to Messi, who has made a movement to receive.

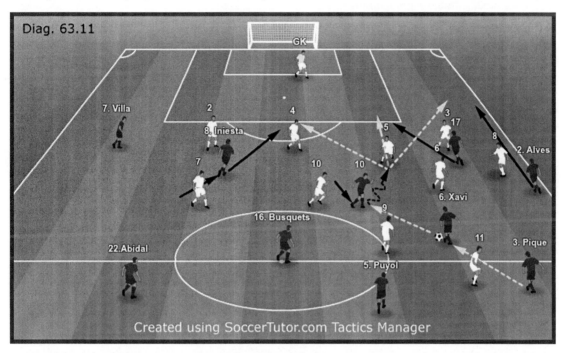

Diag. 63.11

Created using SoccerTutor.com Tactics Manager

As Messi drops back Iniesta moves forward to provide balance.

Messi receives then breaks through the opposition's midfield and reaches the third stage by making the final pass towards Pedro, Iniesta or Alves.

 **ASSESSMENT**

When Messi had the ball at his feet in the opposition half players would make runs into the penalty area or out wide beyond the defensive line.

MESSI MAINTAINING POSSESSION

We have a similar situation on diagram 63.12.

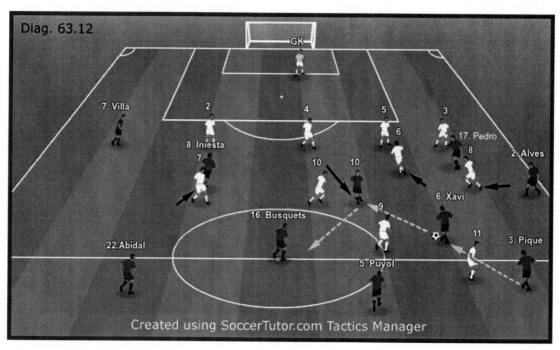

Diag. 63.12

This time white No.6 and No.10 cover the available space for Messi to be able to turn towards the opponent's goal.

As the circumstance does not favour moving on to the third stage, Barcelona focus on retaining the ball via Messi's back pass to Busquets.

MESSI PLAYING FROM THE RIGHT FLANK

Diagram 63.13 up to 63.13.3.

The shift of Messi towards the right side leads Pedro and Alves to move inside, while Iniesta pushes up.

As this attack progresses on diagram 63.13.1, Messi makes a run down the right flank, dribbles past the white No.8 and has to choose between the direct pass to Alves or a driving run towards the centre.

If Messi chooses the driving run, which is a typical movement for him, there are available passing options towards Pedro and Iniesta who move diagonally (Diag.63.13.1B).

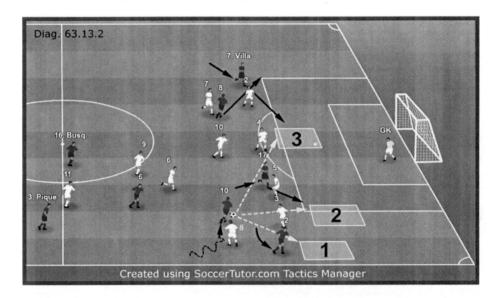

On diagram 63.13.2, Messi receives and immediately makes a run through the gap in midfield.

Villa and Pedro move diagonally, while Alves makes an overlapping run on the right.

Diag. 63.13.3

7. Villa

16. Busq.

3. Pique

GK

Finally on diagram 63.13.3, the same situation is carried out in a different way.

Messi passes to Alves and moves into a supporting position, with the intention of receiving again.

After receiving the pass back from Alves, he continues his run towards the centre, having Pedro and Iniesta as the available passing options.

THE BUILD UP PLAY USING A TWO MAN DEFENCE

When the team used the formation with two central defenders staying at the back, the full backs moved further forward.
The build up play on the right side did not change from when they had three men at the back.

However, the differences between the two formations were remarkable when Barca attacked on the left. This will be analysed in the next chapter.

FORMATIONS

On diagrams 64.1 up to 64.4, the formations used on the right side of the pitch are shown.

The attacking play of Barcelona was based on these formations in order to move the ball to the midfielders or the forwards.

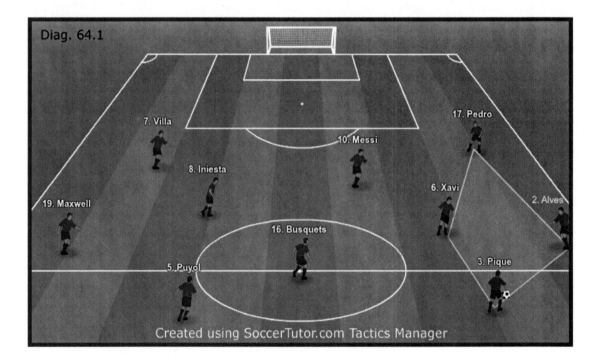

Diag. 64.1

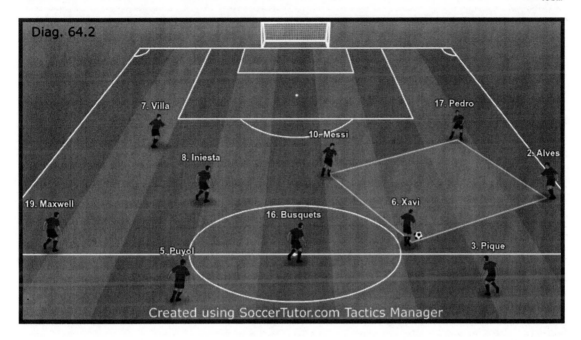

Diag. 64.2

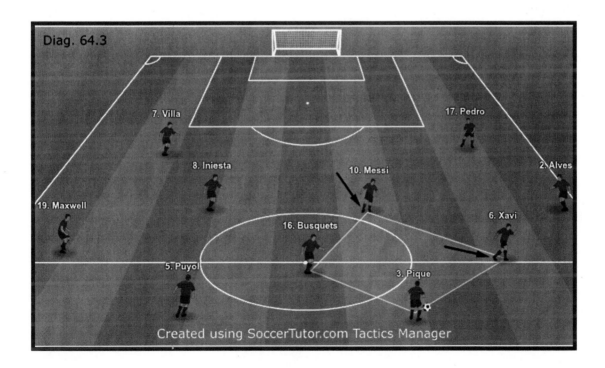

Diag. 64.3

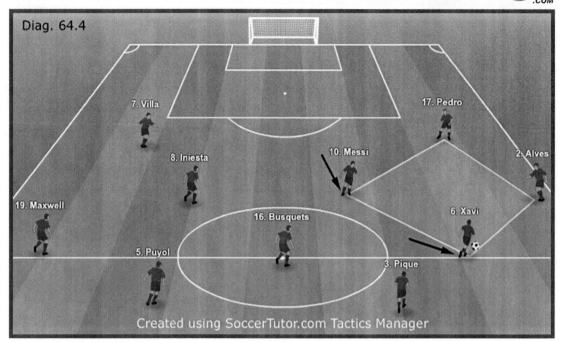

Diag. 64.4

DANIEL ALVES'S PASSING OPTIONS

On diagram 64.5 the available passing options for switching the play are presented.

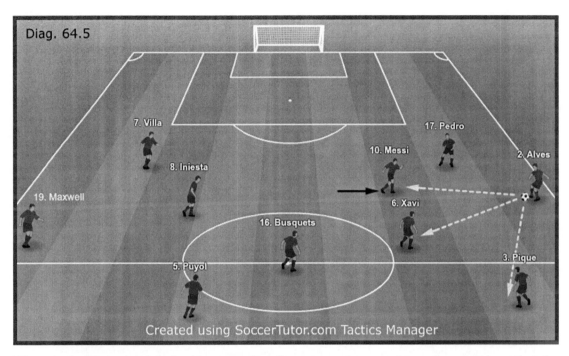

Diag. 64.5

7. Villa
8. Iniesta
19. Maxwell
16. Busquets
5. Puyol
10. Messi
17. Pedro
2. Alves
6. Xavi
3. Pique

Created using SoccerTutor.com Tactics Manager

When the ball is in the right back's possession, there are various passing options inside so that the attacking move is not limited to one side.

The movements and combinations on diagrams 64.1, 64.2 and 64.4 have already been analysed in previous chapters, so this analysis will concern diagram 64.3.

MESSI'S MOVEMENT INTO 'THE HOLE'

On diagrams 65.1 and 65.1.1, Messi drops back to receive the first pass.

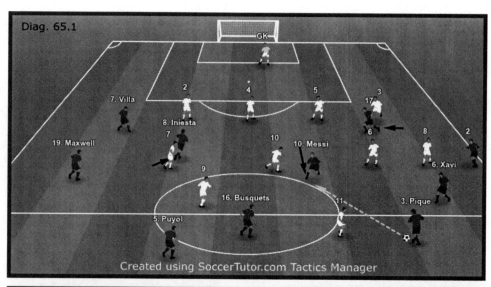

After receiving the ball Messi moves towards the right side, where Pedro creates space for Alves. Messi's pass to Alves moves Barca onto the third stage.

Diag. 65.1.2

On diagram 65.1.2, Messi makes the same movement but the pass to Alves is blocked off by No.8.

Messi then decides to pass to Xavi and moves forward.

Xavi can choose between a pass to Pedro or Pique in order to start the switch of play.

INIESTA ADVANCING INTO MESSI'S POSITION

Diagrams 65.2 and 65.2.1.

Messi receives the ball from Pique and moves towards the left side.

Messi's pass to Iniesta leads to the final stage, with available passing options to Villa, Pedro and Maxwell.

On diagram 65.2.2, the pass is made towards Villa.

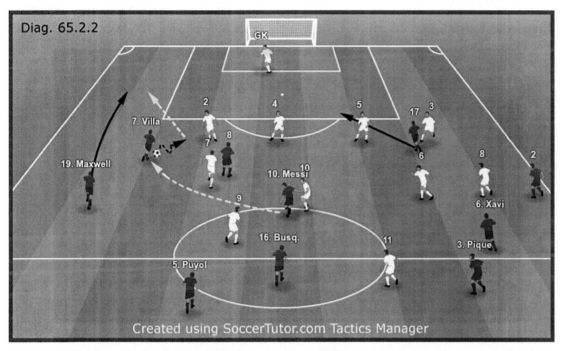

Diag. 65.2.2

GK

2   4   5   17 3

7. Villa

7   8

19. Maxwell

10. Messi
10

9

16. Busq.   11

5. Puyol

6

8   2

6. Xavi

3. Pique

Created using SoccerTutor.com Tactics Manager

Maxwell makes the overlapping run in order to receive the ball in space creating a 2v1 situation which takes place regularly during the attacking play of Barcelona.

ASSESSMENT

Barca's passing combinations and fast movement would often create a 2v1 situation on the flank..

ADVANCING RUNS FROM THE LEFT BACK

Diagrams 65.3 and 65.3.1.

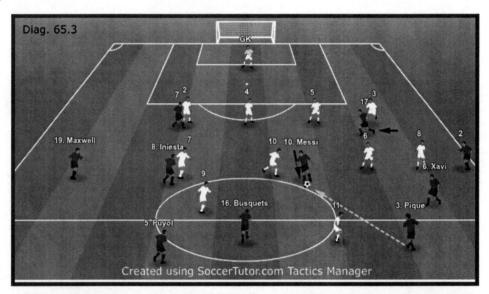

With Villa starting from a more central position, he moves and receives Messi's pass.

Villa can turn towards the opponent's goal or pass back to Messi, who can then pass the ball to Maxwell. It must be mentioned that Maxwell has also moved towards the centre to provide balance for Iniesta's forward run.

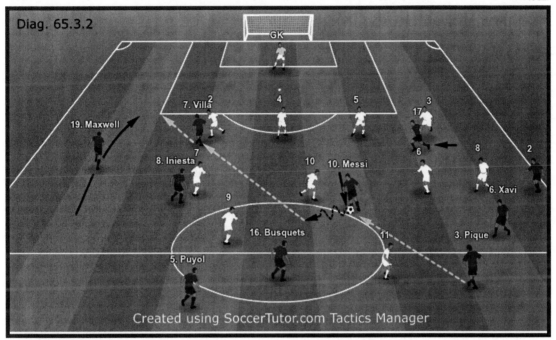

Diag. 65.3.2

Created using SoccerTutor.com Tactics Manager

On diagram 65.3.2, in a similar scenario to diagram's 65.2.2, the ball is directed to Maxwell again through Villa.

 ASSESSMENT

Runs similar to that of Alves' on the right were replicated on the left when Maxwell or Adriano played instead of Abidal.

This was because they were better and technically better in the attacking phase.

MESSI IN THE CENTRAL ZONE

Diagram 65.4.

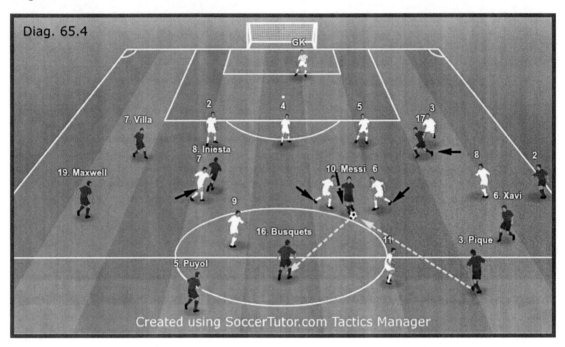

No.10 and No.6 of the opposition prevent Messi from turning.

Possession can only be maintained with a pass back to Busquets.

EXAMPLE 2

Diagrams 65.5 and 65.5.1.

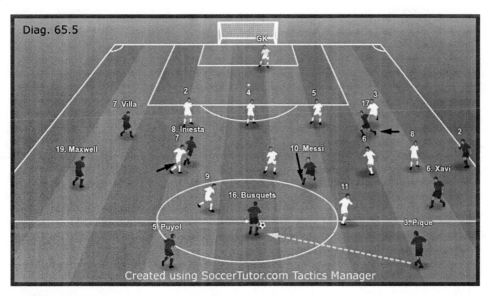

Busquets receives the first pass and as he is under No.9's marking, he passes to Messi who has dropped deep into midfield.

Messi has to choose between the pass towards Pedro, who can then pass to Iniesta which leads to the third stage or the back pass to Xavi which simply helps the team to retain the ball.

SWITCHING PLAY

Diagram 65.6.

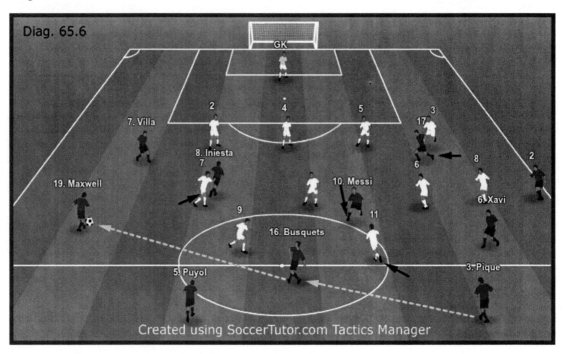

Diag. 65.6

Busquets, after receiving the ball switches the play by passing to Maxwell.

This time the pass towards Messi is being blocked off and the pass towards Iniesta is a risky choice.

 ## ASSESSMENT

The players will not risk losing the ball in the central zone.

There is always a free player to receive the ball of moving to the final stage is not possible.

CHAPTER 9
BARCELONA DURING THE SECOND AND THE THIRD STAGE OF THE ATTACKING PHASE ON THE LEFT SIDE

• **The build up play using the three man defence**..**164**
• **Abidal's passing options**...**166**
• **Attacking down the left flank; 2 v 1**..**169**
• **Overlapping run**...**170**
• **Passing combinations in the final third**..**171**
• **One-twos and diagonal runs in the final third**..**172**
• **Abidal's passing combinations**..**173**
• **Inesta's driving runs**...**175**
• **Movement and the final pass**...**176**
• **2 v 2 on the left flank**..**177**
• **Maintaining possession in tight areas**...**179**
• **Switching the play to the left flank**..**180**

The Build up play using a two man defence...**181**
• **The left back's passing options**...**183**
• **Passing combinations and awareness on the left side**............................**184**
• **2 v 1 on the left flank**..**185**
• **The left back in an advanced position**...**186**
• **Playing out from the back to create a 2 v 1 situation**.............................**188**
• **Awareness and decision making**..**189**
• **Vertical pass from the back**...**190**
• **Switching from the weak side to the strong side**....................................**191**
• **Decision making: Entering the third stage of attack**...............................**192**
• **Switching play from a central position**...**196**
• **Overlapping runs**..**197**
• **Defensive midfielder's passing options**...**199**
• **Iniesta attacking down the left flank**...**200**
• **Timing runs in behind the defence**..**202**
• **Passing through the midfield line**..**203**
• **Switching play from left to right**..**204**

BARCELONA DURING THE SECOND AND THE THIRD STAGE OF THE ATTACKING PHASE ON THE LEFT SIDE

Having analysed some of the ways Barcelona would build up from the right, in this chapter there will be an analysis of the way the team built up play from the left, using either the three or two man defence.

The build up play using the three man defence:

As it has already been mentioned, when the three man defence was used, the team would build up play through the right side of the field most of the time. This was caused by the frequent presence of Lionel Messi and Xavi in this part of the midfield.

Therefore, this side was more crowded during Barcelona's attacking play, so there was often an abundance of space on the left.

These free spaces were used after a fast switching of play from the right towards the left side.

The attacking play on this side was based firstly on the rhombus/diamond, which had the centre back or the defensive midfielder at its base (diagrams 66.1, 66.2 shown on the next page).

And secondly, on the fluid triangle created by the left back (Abidal or Maxwell), the attacking midfielder (Iniesta or Keita) and the wide forward (Villa).

The defensive midfielder during the build up play from this side was extremely important. Busquets provided safety by dropping back and taking up the position of a central defender every time the left sided central defender (Puyol) moved towards the side line in order to give support to the left back, who had moved into a more advanced position (diagram 66.1).

When Puyol was positioned far away from the left back, Busquets moved towards the sideline. This was to take advantage of the free space in order to cover the forward movement.

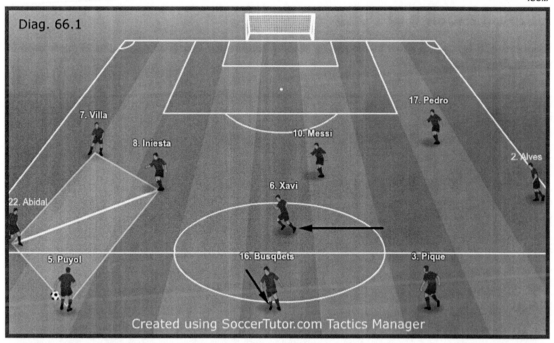

Diag. 66.1

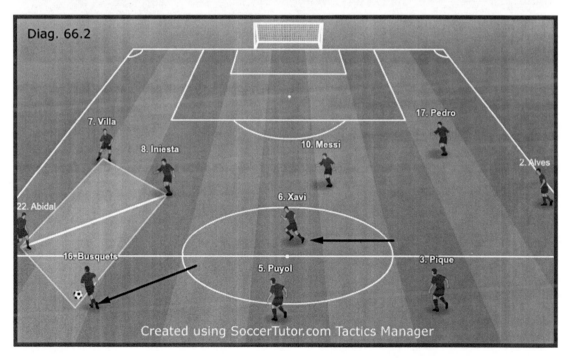

Diag. 66.2

ABIDAL'S PASSING OPTIONS

Diagrams 67.1 up to 67.3 show the available passing options for Abidal when he was in possession in the opponent's half.

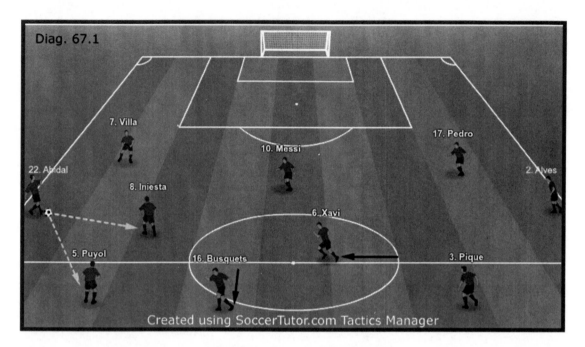

Diag. 67.1

7. Villa

10. Messi

17. Pedro

22. Abidal

2. Alves

8. Iniesta

6. Xavi

5. Puyol

16. Busquets

3. Pique

Created using SoccerTutor.com Tactics Manager

The players take up positions in relation to the defensive midfielder's positioning on the field where he provides safety during the attacking phase.

On diagram 67.1 the ball carrier has two passing options.

One option is to switch play through the midfielders and the second to do the same thing through the defenders.

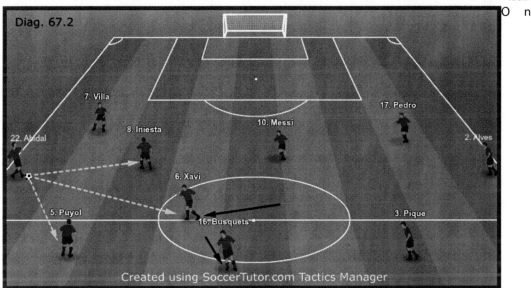

diagram 67.2, Iniesta's advanced position in combination with Busquets taking up a central defender's position causes Xavi to shift towards the strong side to provide one more passing option for the ball carrier.

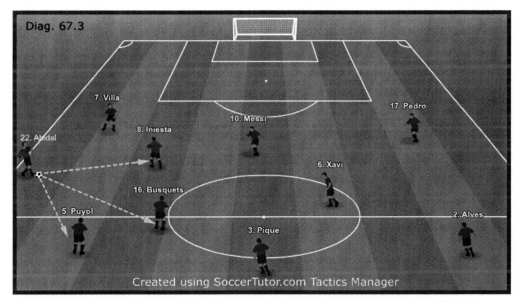

Finally on diagram 67.3, the defensive midfielder takes up his normal position in midfield because there are three players at the back. So, the ball carrier has three available passing options to be able to switch the play.

 ASSESSMENT

Barca would always try to provide the left back with 3 different short passing options.

Busquets' role in this would have to be covered by Xavi if Alves was in an advanced position. This is because Busquets would need to become the third defender.

ATTACKING DOWN THE LEFT FLANK; 2 V 1

On diagram 68.1, the quick forward movement of Abidal after Iniesta's pass creates a 2v1 situation in favour of Barcelona.

Diag. 68.1

Created using SoccerTutor.com Tactics Manager

Villa's cutting run inside the right back No.2 puts him in space to support the ball carrier.

When Villa receives the pass, he will be able to get a low cross into the box.

OVERLAPPING RUN

Diagram 68.2.

Villa makes a movement towards Abidal in order to create a 2v1 situation and use the one-two combination.

ASSESSMENT

Abidal would make forward runs, often combining with Iniesta and Villa.

These were however, more rare than on the right side with Alves.

PASSING COMBINATIONS IN THE FINAL THIRD

On diagram 68.3, Busquets and Messi work the ball to Iniesta.

Diag. 68.3

7. Villa

4

5

3 17. Pedro

10

8

10

2. Alves

6. Xavi

16. Busq.

11

22. Abidal

9

5. Puyol

3. Pique

Created using SoccerTutor.com Tactics Manager

Iniesta passes towards Villa, who because of No.2's movement to cover him, cuts behind the defensive line to receive.

 **ASSESSMENT**

When the opposition's defensive line was compact and well positioned, Villa would pull wide to receive the ball.

ONE-TWOS AND DIAGONAL RUNS IN THE FINAL THIRD

A similar situation is shown on diagram 68.4.

Diag. 68.4

Villa receives the ball and makes a driving run towards the centre to combine with Messi using a one-two or a vertical pass if Messi makes a diagonal run.

Another passing option is provided by Iniesta's overlapping run.

 ASSESSMENT

Barca are able to make passing combinations in very tight spaces because of the players' high technical ability.

David Villa is very quick and good at drifting inside with the ball, which he used to great effect during the 2010-2011 season.

ABIDAL'S PASSING COMBINATIONS

Diagram 68.5.

Abidal passes to Villa and makes a move to receive again.

After receiving the ball, Abidal moves forward and can make a final pass to Messi or Pedro.

EXAMPLE 2

Diagram 68.6.

Iniesta passes to Abidal and attacks the free space while Villa drops back.

So that the ball can be moved to Iniesta there are two possible options:

1) The direct pass to Inesta.

2) The pass to Iniesta via Villa depending on the positioning and movement of the opposition players.

INIESTA'S DRIVING RUNS

Diagram 68.7.

Iniesta moves forward through the gap in the midfield and he has to choose between a diagonal pass to Abidal, to Messi or even Villa.

 ASSESSMENT

Iniesta was an integral link player and would always look to receive the ball in the gap between the midfield and defensive lines of the opposition.

He did this far more than the other midfielders.

MOVEMENT AND THE FINAL PASS

Diagram 68.8.

Diag. 68.8

Created using SoccerTutor.com Tactics Manager

Villa's explosive speed after the first touch enables him to make a driving run towards the centre with two possible passing options:

1) The vertical pass to Messi

2) The diagonal pass to Pedro

 **ASSESSMENT**

Driving runs from the forwards would take defenders out of position and create multiple passing options for the final stage of attack (diagonal runs into the penalty area or out wide).

2 V 2 ON THE LEFT FLANK

Diagram 68.9.

Diag. 68.9

GK

2   4   5   3   10. Messi

7   7   17. Pedro

22   6   8   2. Alves

10   8

8

6

9   11

16. Busq.

5. Puyol   3. Pique

Created using SoccerTutor.com Tactics Manager

The 2v2 situation on the left flank leads Barcelona to focus on retaining Possession.

Villa drops back and helps create a numerical superiority near the ball zone and helps Barca to achieve their aim of keeping the ball.

 **ASSESSMENT**

If numerical superiority could not be achieved Barca would simply maintain possession.).

EXAMPLE 2

On diagram 68.10, there is another 2v2 situation on the left flank.

Here the movement of Iniesta deep takes the No.10 out of position and leaves space on the flank to exploit in behind.

The pass down the line can lead to the final stage as Villa attacks the free space in behind the right back.

✎ ASSESSMENT

As the white defenders keep their central position there is a large gap to the right back, which creates space that Villa can exploit in behind the defensive line.

MAINTAINING POSSESSION IN TIGHT AREAS

Diagram 68.11.

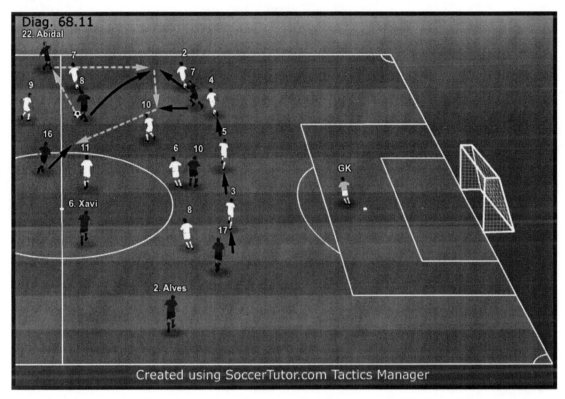

Here there is a quick shift towards the ball zone from the white teams' defenders which prevents Barcelona from creating a numerical superiority.

In this situation the team seeks to retain the ball possession. Villa drops back and Busquets shifts towards the strong side to receive the ball.

 ASSESSMENT

The cohesive shift of the opposition defenders squeezes the play and limits the space for Barca on the left flank.

When there was not a numerical advantage, Busquets or Xavi would shift over to the strong side to provide a passing option.

SWITCHING THE PLAY TO THE LEFT FLANK

On diagram 68.12, Xavi's long pass towards Villa is followed by Abidal's forward movement.

Abidal takes advantage of the transition phase and gains yards forward in order to create a 2v1 situation on the flank.

 ## ASSESSMENT

Barca always had an option wide on the weak side to be used as an outlet.

THE BUILD UP PLAY USING A TWO MAN DEFENCE

When Barcelona used the two man defence the build up on the left was based on the formations shown on diagrams 69.1, 69.2 and 69.3.

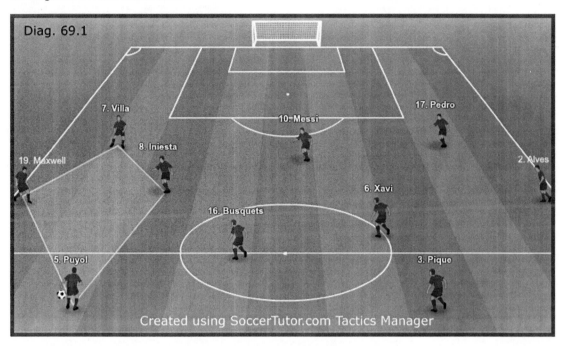

Diag. 69.1

On diagram 69.1 Villa is at the top of the rhombus/diamond.

On diagrams 69.2 and 69.3 Iniesta is at the top of the rhombus.

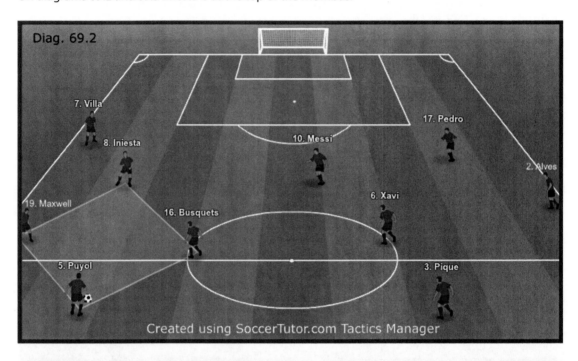

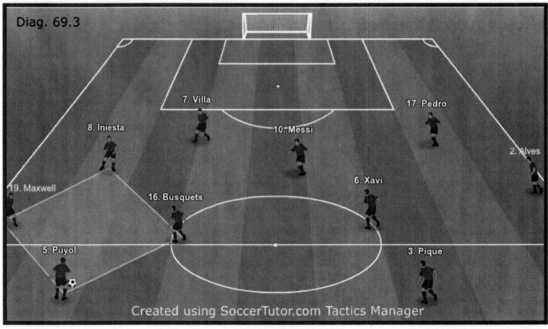

THE LEFT BACK'S PASSING OPTIONS

Diagrams 70.1 and 70.2 show Maxwell's passing options.

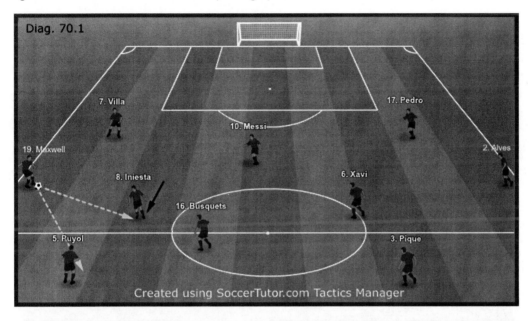

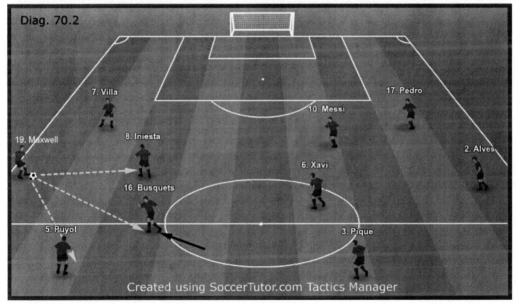

Here the available passing options of the left back are shown where Barcelona can then switch the play from.

PASSING COMBINATIONS AND AWARENESS ON THE LEFT SIDE

Diagrams 71.1 up to 71.9 present situations which are based on the formation depicted on diagram 69.1.

On diagram 71.1, the first pass is made towards Maxwell. There is a 2v2 situation on the flank so the team can risk losing possession by attempting to move on to the third stage. They simply seek to retain the ball.

This is why Villa moves back to receive while Iniesta moves into a more advanced position.

Busquets also moves up to give support to Villa.

The passing options become:

(1) Towards Iniesta (if possible) can lead to the final stage.

(2) Towards Busquets helps the team to retain the ball.

2 V 1 ON THE LEFT FLANK

On diagram 71.2, Maxwell receives the ball and there is a 2v1 situation in favour of Barcelona on the left flank.

Villa makes a diagonal movement towards the sideline in order to receive and get a cross into the box.

 ASSESSMENT

Maxwell would look to get forward more than Abidal, frequently linking up with Villa high up the pitch..

THE LEFT BACK IN AN ADVANCED POSITION

There is a similar situation on diagram 71.3. This time the white teams' defenders move back to deal with Barcelona's numerical superiority.

Maxwell passes to Iniesta and after passing to Messi, Iniesta attacks the free space in behind the defence to receive again from him.

 **ASSESSMENT**

The white team attempt to cope with the many forward runs by dropping deeper to cover.

EXAMPLE 2

On diagram 71.4 Maxwell receives the ball and passes to Iniesta.

Iniesta has three options:

(1) A pass to Villa.

(2) To Messi.

(3) To Busquets.

Diag. 71.4

Created using SoccerTutor.com Tactics Manager

Due to the defensive positioning of the white team the first two options will probably lead to the final stage, while the third one will simply help the retaining of possession.

 **ASSESSMENT**

Iniesta is again pivotal in linking the play and passing to the forwards who can then progress to the final stage.

PLAYING OUT FROM THE BACK TO CREATE A 2 V 1 SITUATION

On diagram 71.5, the first pass is directed to Villa.

Diag. 71.5

Created using SoccerTutor.com Tactics Manager

Villa passes to Maxwell and makes a run inside the right back beyond the defensive line, where he can receive and cross into the penalty area.

 ASSESSMENT

Maxwells' movement forward again helps Barca outnumber the opposition in midfield creating another 2v1 situation..

AWARENESS AND DECISION MAKING

On diagram 71.6, as soon as Villa receives the ball he is being double marked.

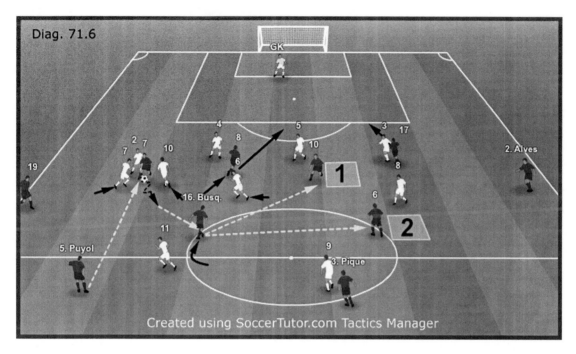

So that Villa can deal with the situation, he moves towards his own goal and passes to Busquets. At the same time Iniesta moves forward.

The new ball carrier (Busquets) can choose between:

(1) Passing to Messi.

(2) Switching the play by passing to Xavi.

The first choice can lead to the final stage, with Pedro and Iniesta being the possible ball receivers.

VERTICAL PASS FROM THE BACK

On diagram 71.7, Puyol makes a vertical pass to Villa.

The defensive positions of the white team's players allow Villa to receive and carry the ball towards the centre where he can combine with Messi.

 ## ASSESSMENT

Puyol's ability to play out from the back here allows Barca to bypass the opposition midfield in a quick and decisive attack.

SWITCHING FROM THE WEAK SIDE TO THE STRONG SIDE

On diagram 71.8, Puyol passes to Iniesta who is under pressure from two opponents.

Diag. 71.8

Created using SoccerTutor.com Tactics Manager

Iniesta has three options:

(1) Pass directly to Busquets.

(2) Receive, move and pass to Xavi.

(3) A long pass to Alves.

ASSESSMENT

The last option leads to numerical superiority on the right flank in favour of Barcelona as Xavi will also shift over creating a 3v2 situation....

DECISION MAKING: ENTERING THE THIRD STAGE OF ATTACK

On diagram 71.9 Puyol has the ball on the left side of defence.

The pass from Puyol is directed to Iniesta, who then passes to Villa.

Villa can pass to Maxwell or Messi, both leading to the final stage.

EXAMPLE 2

On diagrams 72.1 up to 72.7 the situations demonstrated are based on the formation in diagram 69.2.

On diagram 72.1, Maxwell receives the ball from Puyol and passes to Iniesta, who drops deep to receive.

The next pass is aimed towards Villa, who receives and dribbles the ball towards the centre.

This can then lead to the third stage with a pass to Messi in behind the defensive line.

EXAMPLE 3

Diagram 72.2 shows three different options for the ball carrier again.

Due to the white No.10's defensive position, Iniesta has three options:

(1) Pass the ball to Messi (which is difficult because of Iniesta's body position, but it can lead to the third stage).

(2) Pass to Busquets who has pushed forward to receive the ball which enables Barca to retain possession.

(3) Pass to Alves on the right flank which leads to a 2v1 situation and the final stage of the attacking phase.

EXAMPLE 4

On diagram 72.3, Maxwell receives the ball and Busquets moves to give him support for a possible switch of play.

This movement causes Iniesta to push up and Xavi to shift towards the strong side.

Xavi does this in order to provide balance and safety in case the ball possession is lost.
The ball is moved from Maxwell to Iniesta via Villa.

Iniesta can make a final ball towards Pedro or he can combine with Messi using a one-two.

SWITCHING PLAY FROM A CENTRAL POSITION

On diagram 72.4 Puyol passes to Maxwell on the flank.

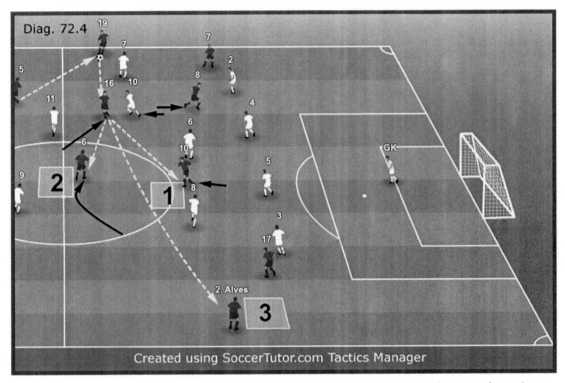

Maxwell's pass is directed to Busquets, but the pressure that is being put on him by No.10 forces him to switch play.

He can achieve this by passing to Messi (option 1), Xavi (option 2) or Alves (option 3).

✎ ASSESSMENT

Alves was an outlet in space for Barcelona a lot of the time.

The attacking formations Barca used gave him the freedom to advance forward and attack at will.

Alves' play down the right flank directly resulted in many goals during the 2010-2011 season....

OVERLAPPING RUNS

On diagram 72.5, Iniesta receives the first pass from Puyol.

Diag. 72.5

Created using SoccerTutor.com Tactics Manager

Iniesta passes to Villa and makes an overlapping run, which gives the ball carrier one more passing option.

Maxwell takes up a position close to the central zone to provide safety and balance.

 ASSESSMENT

Iniesta, Villa and Messi would create a fluid triangle and their combinations were very effective, especially if Messi drifted to the left side.

EXAMPLE 2

Diagram 72.6 starts the same way as 72.5.

There is a similar situation here to the previous one with the difference being that the overlapping run is being made by Maxwell.

 **ASSESSMENT**

The full backs would assess the situation and decide if an advanced run was both necessary and safe, often depending on the positioning of Busquets.

DEFENSIVE MIDFIELDER'S PASSING OPTIONS

On diagram 72.7, Puyol passes to Busquets.

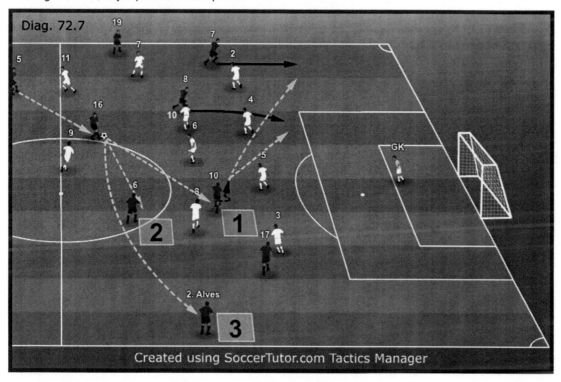

Created using SoccerTutor.com Tactics Manager

Busquets has 3 options:

(1) Pass to Messi, who after making his usual driving run can make a diagonal pass to Iniesta or Villa.

(2) Pass to Xavi

(3) Pass to Alves in an attempt to switch play quickly.

ASSESSMENT

Busquets was able to link with the other midfielders much more when Barca used a two man defence.

INIESTA ATTACKING DOWN THE LEFT FLANK

On diagrams 73.1 up to 73.5, the phases of play demonstrated are based on the formation in diagram 69.3.

On diagram 73.1, Villa's positioning near the central zone leaves free space on the left which is being used by Iniesta, who moves diagonally towards the sideline as soon as Maxwell receives the ball.

Villa shifts towards the strong side to support Iniesta.

Iniesta's next move depends on the movement of David Villa.

Villa has two options:

1) Run in behind the defensive line of the white team, which leads to the third stage.

2) Dropping back and receiving the ball to retain possession for his team.

EXAMPLE 2

On diagram 73.2, the first pass is directed to Iniesta, who drops back to receive the ball.

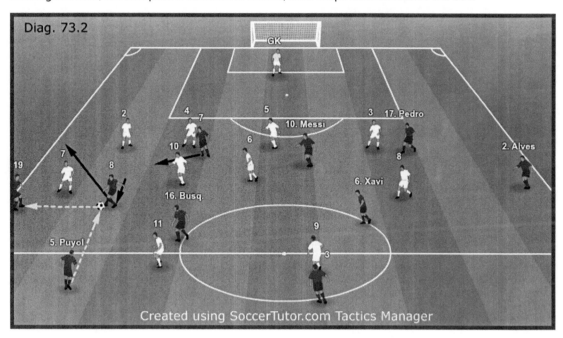

Diag. 73.2

After receiving the ball, Iniesta passes to Maxwell and attacks the free space behind No.7 down the flank.

 **ASSESSMENT**

When Iniesta attacked close to the sideline, Villa would take up a more central position to provide balance..

TIMING RUNS IN BEHIND THE DEFENCE

On diagram 73.3, Iniesta receives and passes to Busquets.

Diag. 73.3

Created using SoccerTutor.com Tactics Manager

The ball is moved through Villa to Messi, who has three available options to make the final pass.

ASSESSMENT

Messi's available options to move into the final stage were made up of the other two forwards' diagonal runs into the penalty area and an advanced run from a full back.

This was typical of Messi's options when in possession in the final third...

PASSING THROUGH THE MIDFIELD LINE

On diagram 73.4, Puyol passes to Busquets and he passes to Iniesta.

Diag. 73.4

Created using SoccerTutor.com Tactics Manager

Villa moves, receives and passes to Maxwell, then seeks to take advantage of the 2v1 situation on the flank by attacking the free space.

ASSESSMENT

Villa made many runs inside the full back and in behind the defensive line....

SWITCHING PLAY FROM LEFT TO RIGHT

Diagram 73.5 shows a successful switch of play.

Diag. 73.5

![ ] **ASSESSMENT**

These movements are quick and often consist of one touch passes.

CHAPTER 10
THE RETAINING OF BALANCE DURING THE ATTACKING PHASE

• Attacking phase formations; 2-5-3 207
• Attacking phase formations; 3-4-3 209
• Defensive midfielder's role 211
• The full back's role 214
• Maintaining balance; Forwards 216
• Maintaining balance; Left side 218

THE RETAINING OF BALANCE DURING THE ATTACKING PHASE

Barcelona became one of the world's most loved sides because of the unique way the team performed during the attacking phase.

A team, in order to be successful must not only play attractive football, but also win trophies. For that reason, the attractive style of football during the attacking phase is not enough.

A very important issue for combining the spectacular performances with winning games is the retaining of the team's balance during the attacking phase.

The retaining of balance helps the team to make an effective transition from attack to defence and provides safety, especially when the ball possession is lost.

The teams' balance is a result of good collective work, the cooperation between the players as well as the discipline in their duties.

In this chapter some of the movements made in combination to provide balance and safety to the team will be demonstrated.

These movements made during the match may not be visible to the average spectator, but they are basic and essential elements of Barcelona's play.

ATTACKING PHASE FORMATIONS: 2-5-3

Diagrams 74.1 up to 74.3 show situations where Barcelona used a two man defence during the build up play.

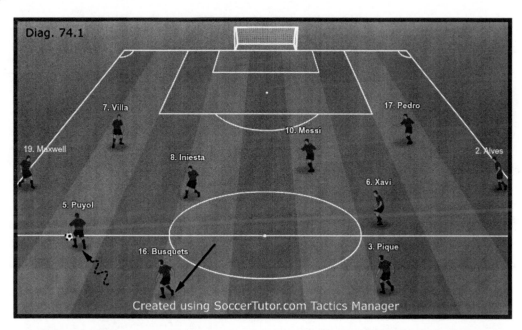

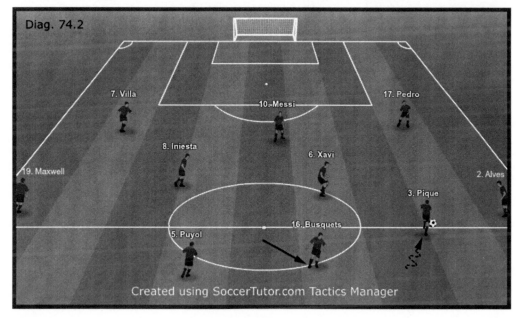

Diag. 74.3

7. Villa

10. Messi

17. Pedro

8. Iniesta

6. Xavi

19. Maxwell

3. Pique

2. Alves

16. Busquets

5. Puyol

Created using SoccerTutor.com Tactics Manager

These situations show how the defensive midfielder restores the team's balance during the attacking phase when the central defenders move forward with the ball.

ATTACKING PHASE FORMATIONS: 3-4-3

On diagrams 75.1 up to 75.3 the team is shown using the three man defence.

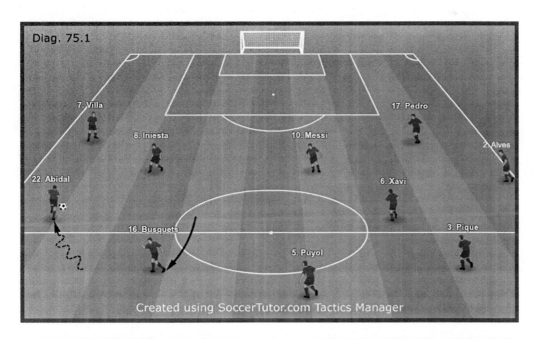

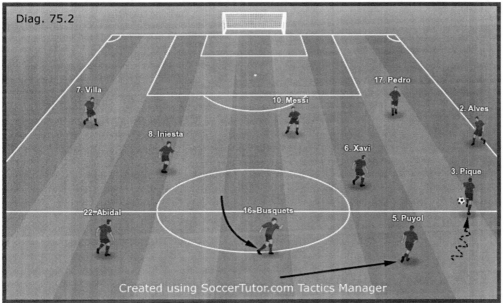

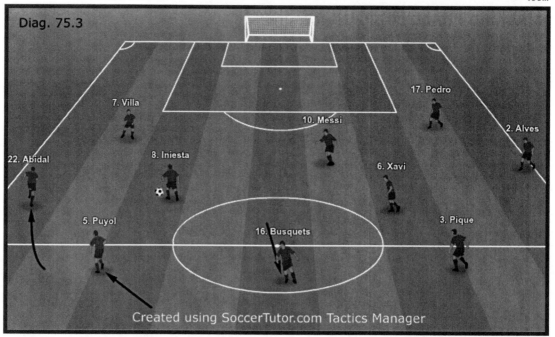

Diag. 75.3

The defensive midfielder is the one who covers the gaps created by the forward runs of any of the three defenders, both with the ball (75.1, 75.2) or without the ball (75.3).

DEFENSIVE MIDFIELDER'S ROLE

The defensive midfielder has an important role in providing numerical superiority in the defensive zone.

The outnumbering of the opponents at the back led the remaining defenders to defend actively when the loss of possession took place.

This behaviour during the transition phase resulted in the immediate regaining of possession where Barcelona could then start another attack.

Diagrams 76.1 and 76.2 show the defensive midfielder's positioning when Barcelona faced teams using two or one forward respectively.

In the first situation the defensive midfielder takes up a position close to the opponent's forward who is in the less advanced position.

Diag. 76.2

Here on Diagram 76.2 Busquets is positioned close to Barcelona's two attacking midfielders ready to react quickly to a possible loss of possession.

With Busquets' position he could close down white No.8 or No.10 if they intercept the ball.

Diag. 76.3

When the team used the three man defence, the safety provided by the three defenders allowed the defensive midfielder to focus on supporting the two attacking midfielders (diagram 76.3).

ASSESSMENT

With two defenders, Busquets' prime concern was for the defensive balance of the team.

When three defenders were used he could be much more active in the attacking phase, taking part in passing combinations.

THE FULL BACK'S ROLE

A very important issue in retaining the team's balance was the timing of the forward runs from the full backs, which was especially important when the team were using a two man defence.

The full backs made their movements forward when there was clear possession for Barca's midfielders and only when the attacking midfielders were in a position to provide support for them.

In each different phase of play, the full backs would maintain a short enough distance from the opposition midfielders so they were still able to form their defensive positions if possession was lost.

On diagram 77.1 Barca have possession of the ball with Iniesta in a supporting position to Maxwell.

The two full backs move up the field to more advanced positions while still remaining close to the opposing wide midfielders.

On Diagram 77.2, Xavi does not have clear possession of the ball as he is under pressure from white No.8. Maxwell and Alves maintain their deeper position to cover the wide midfielders.

This enables them to put immediate pressure on these players if possession is lost.

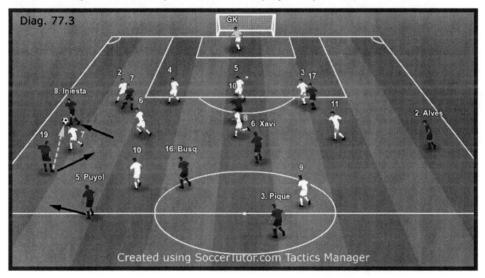

On diagram 77.3, Iniesta has clear possession of the ball, but he is not close enough to the left back Maxwell.

To close the gap, Maxwell after his pass to Iniesta, moves towards the centre to provide safety and balance, while Puyol moves into a supporting position to receive the ball.

MAINTAINING BALANCE; FORWARDS

The team's balance was lost in some other cases. There were countless times during the season where Messi dropped deep into midfield.

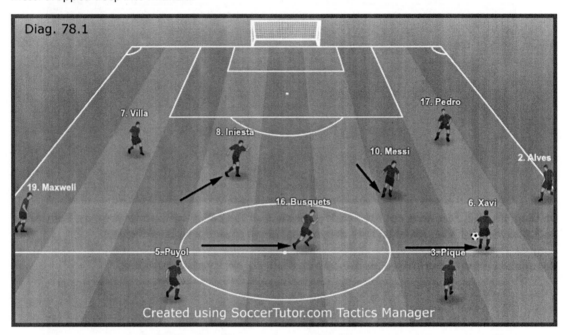

Diag. 78.1

When this took place on the right (majority of the time), Iniesta moved from the left side to take over Messi's role up front.

In these instances Iniesta would make the killer pass or act as the team's third forward.

Diag. 78.2

When Messi dropped back on the left side, Xavi moved further up field on the right to provide attacking balance (diagram 78.2).

MAINTAINING BALANCE; LEFT SIDE

The retaining of balance was necessary during the build up play on the left side as Busquets would drop deep to take up the position of a central defender.

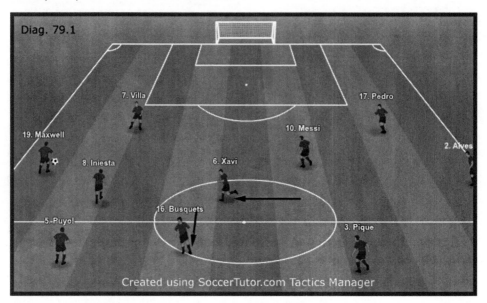

In these situations Xavi moved towards the strong side to give support for a possible switch of play (diag. 79.1).

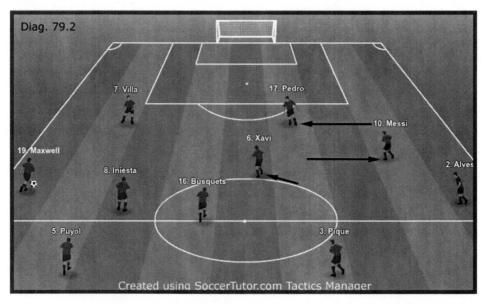

On diagram 79.2, Messi's shift towards the right causes Pedro to move towards the centre.

CHAPTER 11
THE TRANSITION FROM ATTACK TO DEFENCE

• The safety player 221
• Applying immediate pressure when possession is lost 229
• Busquets as the safety player..230
• Using three men at the back..232
• Possession lost near the opposing penalty area 234
• Winning the ball back in the central zone 236
• Regaining possession near the sideline 240
• Regaining possession near to the opponent's penalty area......................................243
• Cohesion in the transition phase 245
• When immediate regaining of possession is not possible..246
• When immediate regaining of possession is possible..248
• Regaining possession in the centre of the field 249
• Team cohesion to regain possession 250
• Winning the ball in an advanced wide position..253
• The opposition win the ball near the halfway line 255
• Preventing the switch of play 258
• Using two safety players...259

THE TRANSITION FROM ATTACK TO DEFENCE

The way the team moved on from the first stage of their attack up to the third was without doubt spectacular and could break down even the best and most organised defensive teams.

However, the way the team made the transition from attack to defence was equally as impressive.

The speed in which the players acted during the transition, together with the immediate physical and psychological pressure put on the opponents, resulted in Barcelona's dominance in every single game. The way the team acted during this phase was related to the formation used in the attacking play.

The players played differently when the team used three men at the back (diagram 55.1) compared to when the team used a two man defence (diagram 55.2).

There were five elements that contributed to Barca's effectiveness during the transition from attack to defence:

a) Compactness; maintaining short distances between the players.

b) Retaining the team's balance during the attacking phase (analysed in the previous chapter).

c) The constant presence of a safety player in every attacking move.

d) The quick reaction of the players when the ball possession was lost.

e) The decisive contribution of the defensive midfielder.

This phase is key to Barcelona's tactics as it helps them win the ball back immediately after losing it.

As Barca applied the pressure high up the pitch many of their most effective attacks were formed from these situations.

THE SAFETY PLAYER

Diagrams 80.1 up to 80.9 show the positions of the safety player/s on the field during the attacking phase when the team used a two man defence respectively.

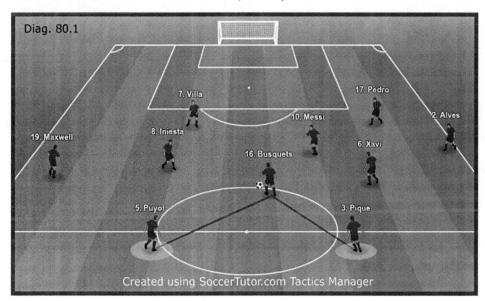

80.1: The safety players are Puyol and Pique.

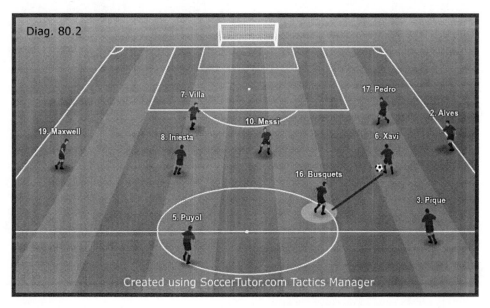

80.2: The safety player is Busquets.

Diag. 80.3

80.3: The safety player is Xavi.

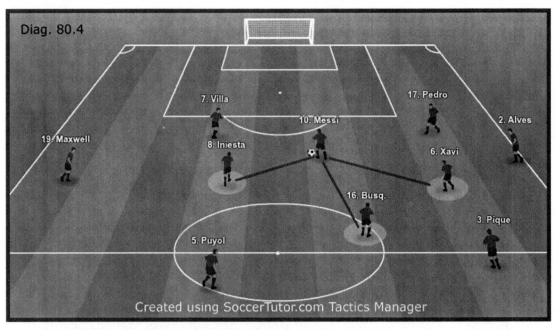

Diag. 80.4

80.4: The safety players are Busquets, Xavi and Iniesta.

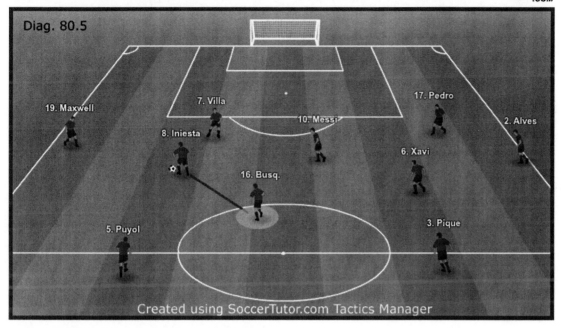

80.5: The safety player is Busquets.

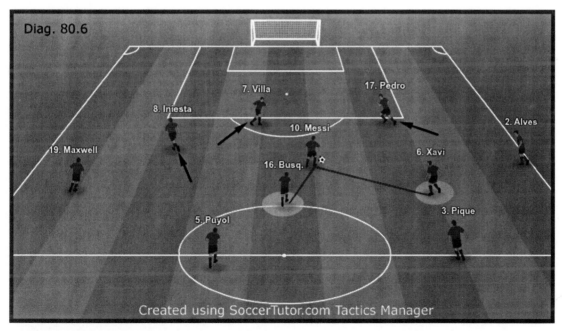

80.6: The safety players are Busquets and Xavi.

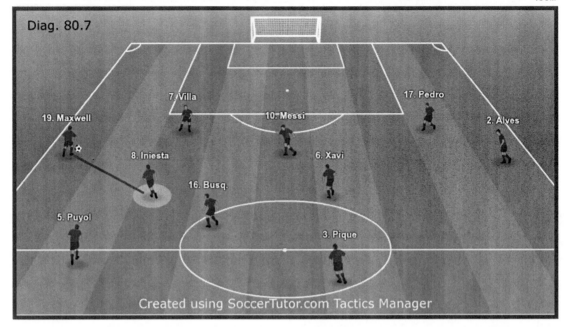

80.7: The safety player is Iniesta.

80.8: The safety player is Maxwell.

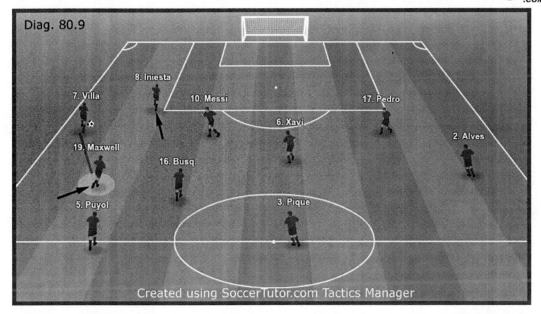

80.9: The safety player is Maxwell.

Diagrams 81.1 up to 81.7 show the positions of the safety player/s on the field during the attacking phase when the team used a two man defence respectively.

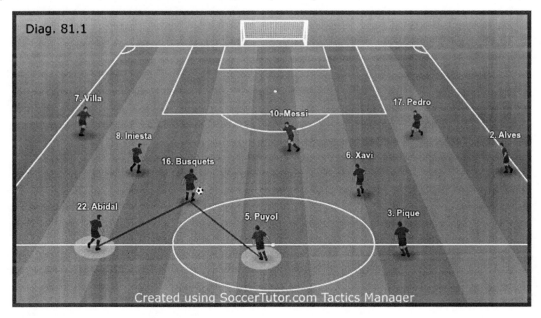

81.1: The safety players are Puyol and Abidal.

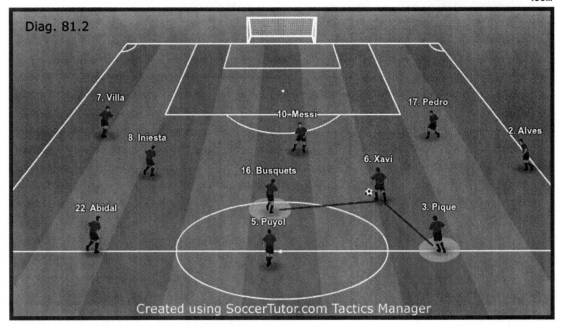

81.2: The safety players are Pique and Busquets.

81.3: The safety player is Xavi.

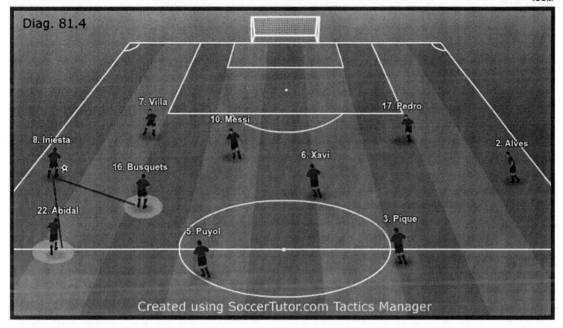

81.4: The safety players are Abidal and Busquets.

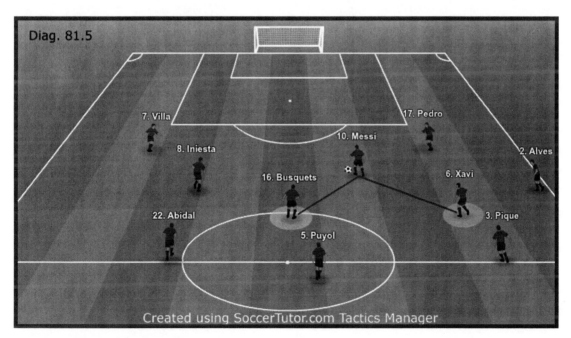

81.5: The safety players are Busquets and Xavi.

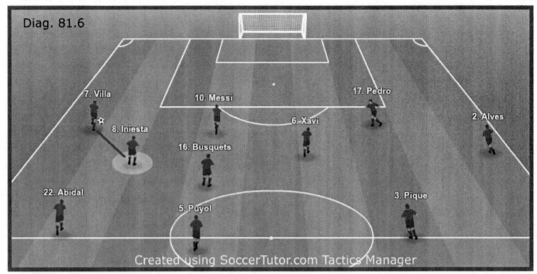

81.6: The safety player is Iniesta.

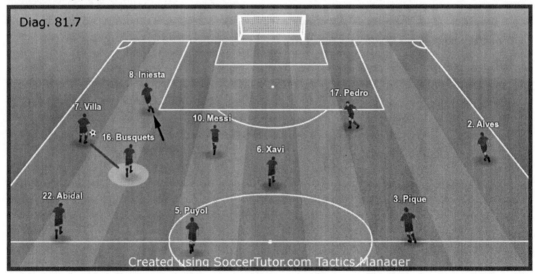

81.7: The safety player is Busquets.

The role of the safety player is extremely important as he has two responsibilities.

He gives support behind the ball in order to provide an available passing option for the ball carrier, and he also provides safety.

The safety is provided by taking immediate action in case the ball carrier loses possession.

APPLYING IMMEDIATE PRESSURE WHEN POSSESSION IS LOST

Diagrams 82.1 shows Xavi lose possession.

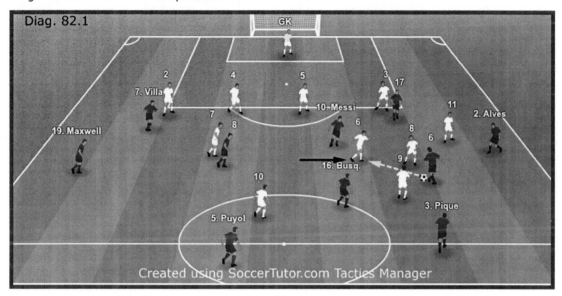

Here we show the decisive contribution of the defensive midfielder in a two man defence after the loss of possession.

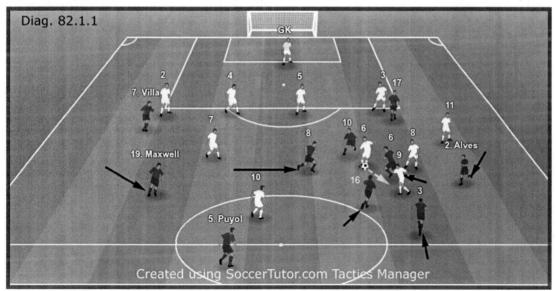

The immediate pressure on the new ball carrier No.8 is being applied by Xavi and Iniesta, while Busquets moves close to No.9 and is ready to apply pressure if the ball is directed to him. (Diag.82.1.1)

BUSQUETS AS THE SAFETY PLAYER

On diagrams 82.2 white No.6 intercepts the ball.

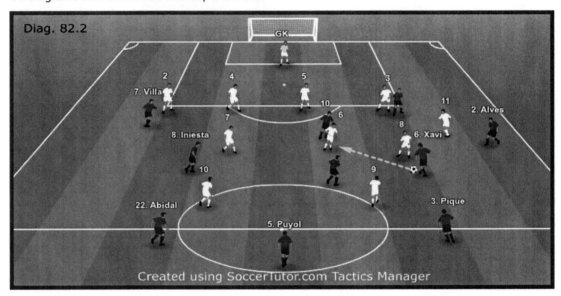

Busquets plays in front of a three man defence and focuses on giving support and safety for Xavi.

After the loss of possession, Busquets is the first one to put pressure on the ball carrier and is supported by Xavi and Iniesta, while Pique moves close to No.9 and Abidal close to No.10. (Diag. 82.2.1)

ASSESSMENT

Barca would close down the ball carrier when they lost possession, but would also make sure to put pressure on all the possible ball receivers.

This made sure that Barca could prevent any build up play from the opposition to ensure they won the ball back as quickly as possible.

USING THREE MEN AT THE BACK

On diagrams 83.1 and 83.1.1 there is an analysis of the transition phase from attack to defence when the three man defence was used.

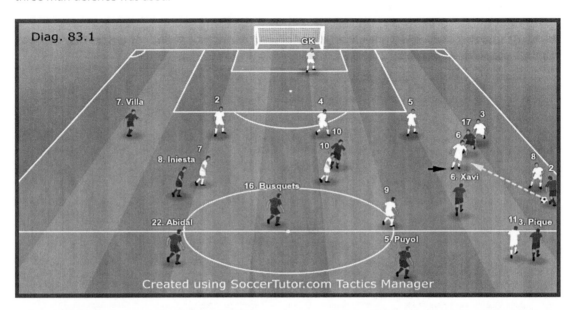

After the loss of possession when No.6 intercepts the ball, the first man putting pressure on the new ball carrier is the safety player (Xavi). Alves moves towards the centre and helps doubles up on No.6.

The ball carrier is being completely blocked with the contribution of Pedro and Messi added.

Pique reduces his distance from No.11 and he is ready to take action if there is a possible pass directed to him.

Busquets moves to mark the other forward (No.9), who is positioned further up the field.

 **ASSESSMENT**

Barca were extremely quick to close down the ball carrier preventing their opponents having any time to think when on the ball.

POSSESSION LOST NEAR THE OPPOSING PENALTY AREA

Diagrams 83.2 and 83.2.1 show Barcelona's transition phase when the possession is lost near the opposition's penalty area.

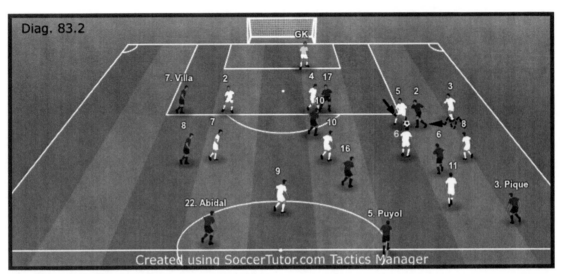

The white team's No.5 wins the ball and passes to No.10.

The immediate pressure is applied by Busquets, Iniesta and Messi, while Xavi helps block off an available passing option for the ball carrier.

Pique and Abidal mark the possible receivers No.9 and No.11 very tightly, while Puyol covers both of them as he is the spare man at the back.

ASSESSMENT

By covering the possible passes of the ball carrier Barca prevent the opposition from moving through the attacking phases.

Preventing these passes meant the opposition could not get out of their half.

When Barca inevitably won the ball back they were often in a great position to reach the final stage of attack themselves.

WINNING THE BALL BACK IN THE CENTRAL ZONE

Diagrams 83.3 and 83.3.1.

The interception of the ball is made by the white team's No.5.

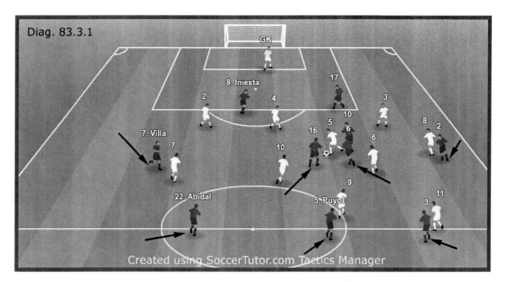

The safety players Busquets and Xavi try to put immediate pressure in order to block No.5's passing options.

Villa moves towards the centre and close to No.7. Puyol reduces his distance to No.9 without marking him closely, while Pique and Abidal move towards the centre as well.

EXAMPLE 2

On diagrams 83.4 and 83.4.1, No.10 wins the ball.

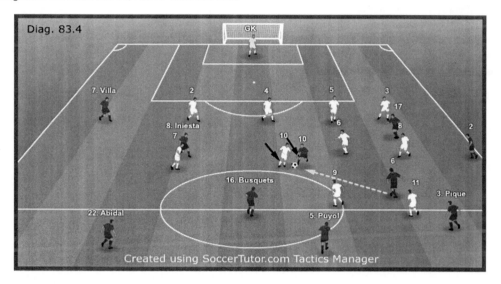

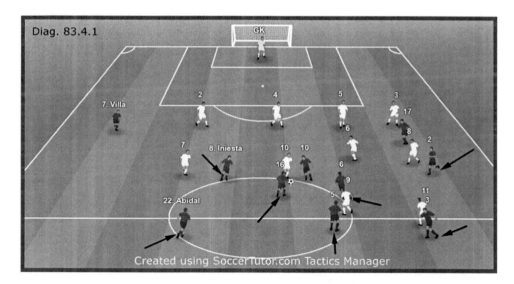

Busquets becomes the first defender by putting pressure on No.5, while Iniesta and Xavi move to block the ball in the central zone.

Pique and Puyol move to mark No.9 and No.11 tightly.

ASSESSMENT

All the players tuck in as the ball is in the central zone.

This creates a numerical advantage, making it far easier to regain possession.

Another attack can then be launched..

EXAMPLE 3

Diagrams 83.5 and 83.5.1.

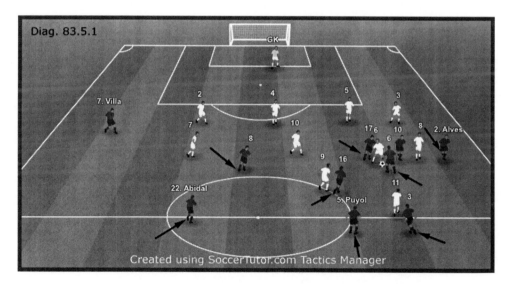

During Messi's driving run towards the centre, No.6 intercepts the ball. Xavi, (the safety player) is the first to put pressure on him, as Pedro helps double up.

Busquets and Pique mark the possible ball receivers No.9 and No.11 closely.

REGAINING POSSESSION NEAR THE SIDELINE

On Diagram 83.6, Messi makes a run with the ball down the flank.

No.5 contests Messi, intercepts the ball and passes to No.6.

Xavi (the safety player) puts pressure on No.6 in order to hold him close to the sideline, while Pique gives cover to Xavi by moving forward.

EXAMPLE 2

On diagrams 83.7 and 83.7.1, the attacking move takes place on the left.

Abidal's pass to Villa is intercepted by white No.2.

The safety player (Iniesta) moves to put pressure on No.2 and at the same time he seeks to cover the pass towards No.7.

Busquets, who has already dropped back to cover Abidal's forward run, marks No.9 closely and Puyol moves forward to give cover to Iniesta.

 ASSESSMENT

When possession is lost near the sideline the Barcelona players shift over to create a numerical advantage and prevent the opposition from playing inside and switching play.

When this numerical advantage is achieved winning the ball back is inevitable and Barca often use this advantage to reach the third stage of attack.

REGAINING POSSESSION NEAR TO THE OPPONENT'S PENALTY AREA

Diagrams 83.8 and 83.8.1 show a phase of play on the edge of the penalty area.

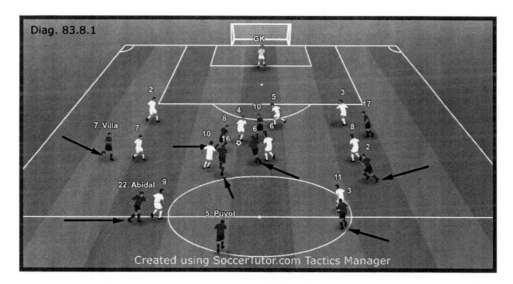

After the ball interception by white No.4, Xavi and Iniesta double mark the new ball carrier, while Busquets is ready to prevent a possible pass towards No.10.

Abidal and Pique mark the two forwards closely in order to block off a possible pass directed to them.

 ASSESSMENT

The movement is again to cover possible passes and for the team to move inwards together to limit space and create a numerical advantage around the ball zone.

COHESION IN THE TRANSITION PHASE

On diagram 83.9 and 83.9.1, No.2 intercepts the ball.

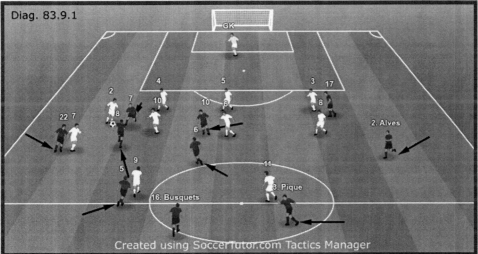

Immediately he is under Iniesta's (safety player) and Villa's pressure, while Messi, Xavi and Abidal also move towards the ball carrier. Lastly Puyol marks No.9 closely.

 ## ASSESSMENT

As all the players move close to the ball zone all possible options are removed and Barca will inevitably regain possession.

WHEN IMMEDIATE REGAINING OF POSSESSION IS NOT POSSIBLE

On diagram 83.10, the pass from Iniesta is intercepted by No.2.

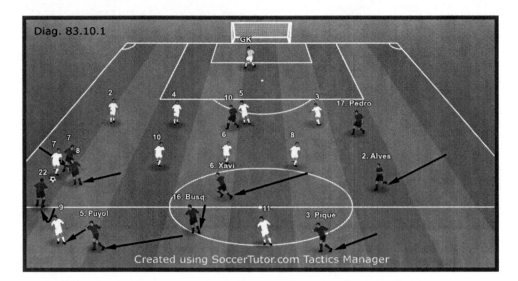

Because of the fact that the safety player (Iniesta) is unable to apply immediate pressure, Barcelona's defenders drop off in order to limit the space behind the defensive line. This movement gives Busquets the appropriate time to move back and give support to the defenders. (Diag. 83.10.1)

Iniesta becomes the first defender and seeks to keep the ball carrier near the sideline.

Villa moves towards the centre while Abidal drops back to block off a possible pass towards No.9 who has made a diagonal run.

Then Abidal pushes up to help double mark the ball carrier.

 # ASSESSMENT

When immediate pressure is not possible the defence drop deeper to cover the forward's runs and allow the team time to balance again.

WHEN IMMEDIATE REGAINING OF POSSESSION IS POSSIBLE

Diagrams 83.11 and 83.11.1.

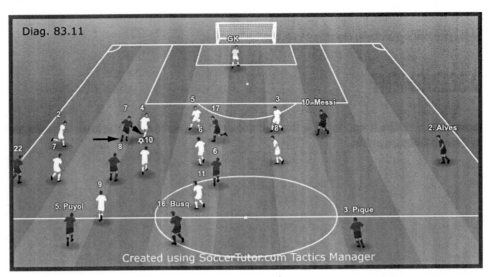

During Villa's driving run towards the centre, No.4 pressures him and intercepts the ball.

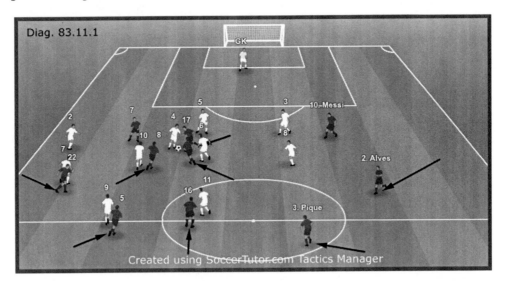

Pedro's reaction is immediate as he applies pressure, while at the same time Iniesta and Xavi move towards the ball carrier blocking his available options. Busquets and Puyol close down No.11 and No.9 respectively, while Abidal moves to intercept a possible pass towards

---

REGAINING POSSESSION IN THE CENTRE OF THE FIELD

On diagrams 84.1 and 84.1.1, the ball is intercepted by white No.10.

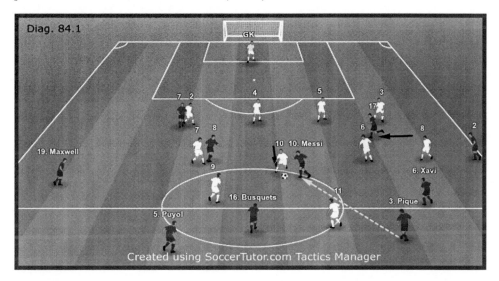

Busquets, being the safety player, applies pressure and at the same time he covers the possible pass towards No.9.

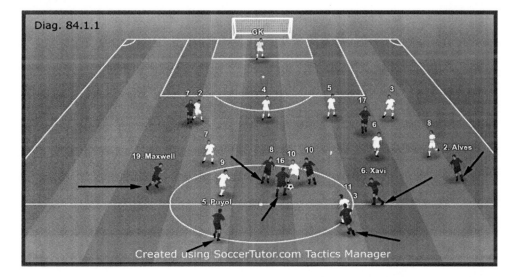

Busquets' immediate action gives Iniesta time to take up a defensive position and for Xavi to drop back by moving towards the centre. Pique marks No.11 closely because he is a possible ball receiver.

TEAM COHESION TO REGAIN POSSESSION

On diagrams 84.2 and 84.2.1, Xavi's pass is intercepted by No.5.

Messi (the safety player) puts pressure on him while Xavi and Alves are ready to prevent a possible pass towards No.6 and No.8 respectively.

Finally, Pique and Busquets are ready to double team No.11 in case the pass is directed to him.

EXAMPLE 2

Diagrams 84.3 and 84.3.1.

No.6 becomes the new ball carrier.

Busquets moves to contest him immediately and Xavi (the second safety player) moves towards No.6 to carry out double marking. The full backs move towards the centre and Pique shortens his distance from No.11.

EXAMPLE 3

Diagrams 84.4 and 84.4.1.

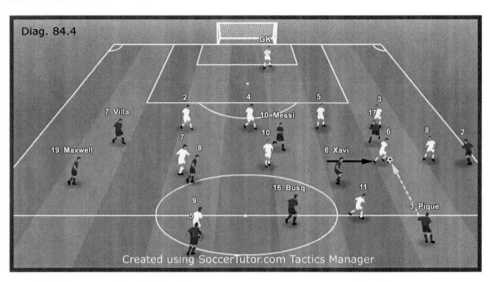

No.6 intercepts Pique's pass towards Pedro.

Xavi (the safety player) puts pressure on him, while Alves seeks to double mark No.6 by moving towards the centre. Busquets marks No.11 closely and Pique moves up to give support to Busquets in case the pass is directed to No.11.

WINNING THE BALL IN AN ADVANCED WIDE POSITION

Diagrams 84.5 and 84.5.1.

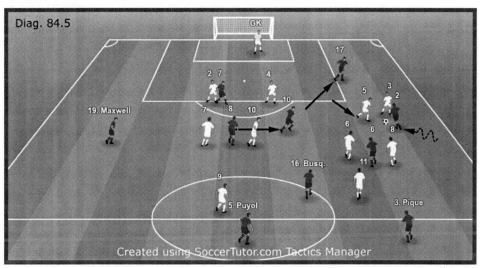

The possession for Barcelona is lost after Alves' driving run towards the centre.

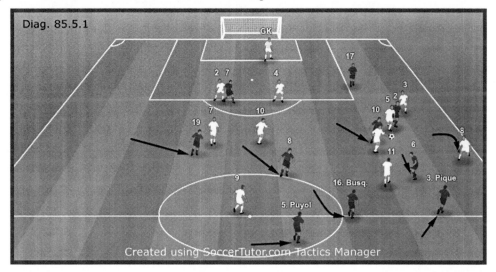

The new ball carrier (white No.5) is not being put under Xavi's (safety player) pressure because a possible pass towards No.8, who moves near the sideline would leave him out of position.

Xavi keeps a safe distance from No.5 in order to mark both No.5 and No.8.

Messi puts pressure on No.5 seeking to force him towards the sideline, while Pique moves forward and shortens his distance to No.8 to be able to prevent a possible pass towards him.

 ASSESSMENT

Immediate pressure is not possible so the team cover the options to provide defensive balance.

THE OPPOSITION WIN THE BALL NEAR THE HALFWAY LINE

Diagrams 84.6 and 84.6.1.

The pass towards Maxwell is intercepted by No.7 who moves forward. Iniesta (the safety player) is the first one to put pressure on No.7.

Puyol drops back, giving time for Busquets and Alves to recover their positions. This then creates superiority in numbers at the back in favour of Barca.

As soon as the numerical superiority is achieved, Puyol moves forward to double mark the ball carrier together with Iniesta.

EXAMPLE 2

Diagrams 84.7 and 84.7.1.

No.7 intercepts Puyol's pass.

Iniesta puts pressure on him and Maxwell moves to carry out double marking.

Busquets moves to mark No.11, while also blocking a possible pass towards him.

EXAMPLE 3

Diagrams 84.8 and 84.8.1 show a situation after Barca lose possession.

Busquets puts pressure on the ball and Maxwell moves in order to apply double marking.

Puyol closes down No.11, while Pique moves to provide balance and Alves tracks back to create superiority in numbers in defence.

PREVENTING THE SWITCH OF PLAY

On diagram 84.9 white No.4 wins a 1v1 against Villa.

Iniesta (the safety player) applies immediate pressure. Pedro moves towards the centre and together with Alves who moves close to No.8 seek to prevent the available passing options for switching the play. (Diag.84.9.1)

Maxwell and Xavi try to mark the possible ball receivers, while Busquets moves near to the ball zone and covers the pass towards No.9 as well.

USING TWO SAFETY PLAYERS

Finally we have diagrams 84.10 and 84.10.1.

Iniesta and Busquets (both safety players) react immediately and double mark the ball carrier.

As Busquets moves forward, Xavi is the one who provides balance and Maxwell helps create a numerical superiority at the back.

CHAPTER 12
THE TRANSITION FROM DEFENCE TO ATTACK

• Pressing near the sidelines in an advanced position 262
• Transition to the final attacking stage 266
• Intercepting a pass from the goalkeeper 271

THE TRANSITION FROM DEFENCE TO ATTACK

Barcelona traditionally seek to dominate the game against every opposing team by controlling possession.

That is why the team's pressing is applied high up the field and close to the opponent's penalty area, and seeks to get the ball back as soon as possible.

This style of play forces the opposition to a passive role during the whole ninety minutes.

Opposing teams rarely build up from the back using short passes because the opposition is afraid of losing possession when many of its players are above the line of the ball.

The regaining of possession usually took place when most of the opposition's players were behind the line of the ball and with Barcelona having no available free space to use. In such cases, Barcelona's players chose to build up patiently in order to find the right time to move onto the final stage of the attacking phase.

There were of course situations when the regaining of possession took place when many opponents were out of defensive positions (above the line of the ball), with Barcelona seeking to carry out a quick transition to attack. In those cases the team's players used fast forward runs with the ball and direct vertical and diagonal passes towards the forwards (Pedro, Villa, Messi).

These instances where the opposing team did try and play a passing game building up from the back are shown on the diagrams to follow. Barcelona could utilise these situations to make a very quick transition from defence to attack.

PRESSING NEAR THE SIDELINES IN AN ADVANCED POSITION

On diagram 85.1 the application of pressing ends with David Villa's interception..

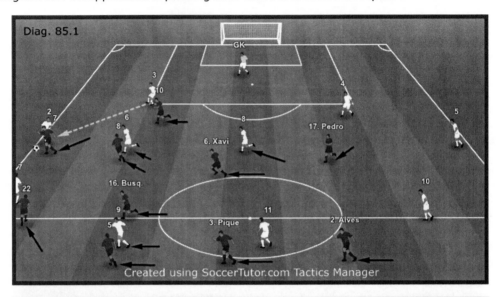

Villa moves forward and creates a 3v2 situa t ion. The pass is made to Messi who has the options of passing to Pe dro a nd Villa or moving forward and shoot ing at goa l.
(Diag. 85.1.1)

ASSESSMENT

Villa's body shape is important here.

He closes the potential passing options for the ball carrier enabling himself to regain possession more easily.

When he carries the ball forward Barca quickly enter the final stage of attack.

EXAMPLE 2

Diagrams 85.2 up to 85.2.2 show a similar situation to the previous one.

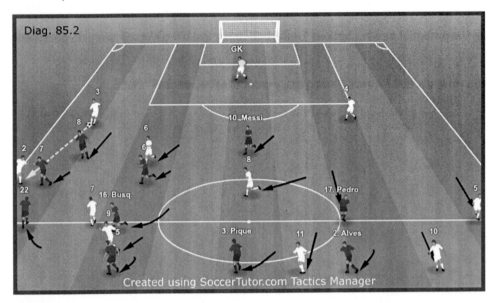

During the pressing application, the ball is directed to white No.2 who is positioned near the sideline. No.2 is being double marked by Abidal and Villa, with the first one intercepting the ball.

Diag. 85.2.2

Created using SoccerTutor.com Tactics Manager

Abidal passes to Villa and Villa to Iniesta. Iniesta makes the killer pass towards Messi who moves diagonally between the two central defenders.

 ASSESSMENT

Pressing high up the pitch again enabled rapid entry to the final stage when possession was regained.

TRANSITION TO THE FINAL ATTACKING STAGE

Diagrams 85.3 up to 85.3.2 show a transition.

The pass is directed to white No.6 who is positioned in the centre of the field.

No.6 is being triple marked by Villa, Iniesta and Xavi.

Xavi intercepts the ball and moves forward.

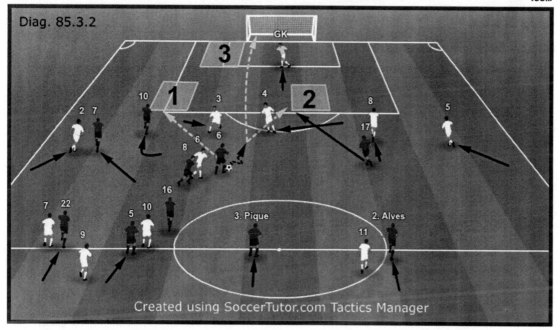

Diag. 85.3.2

As the two opposing central defenders move towards the centre, Xavi has three options:

1) The pass to Messi is very likely to happen

2) A forward run with the ball and the pass to Pedro

3) A forward run which ends with a shot at goal.

 **ASSESSMENT**

When Barcelona press so high up the pitch the rewards are great when they win possession, as the final/decisive ball can be played.

EXAMPLE 2

Diagram 85.4 shows the pass to No.11.

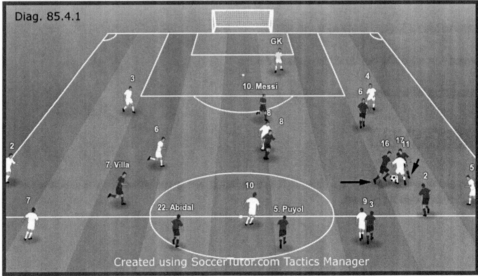

Busquets and Pedro double mark the ball carrier. Busquets intercepts the ball and passes to Pedro who runs into the free space on the right and receives.

Diag. 85.4.2

Created using SoccerTutor.com Tactics Manager

Pedro moves forward and delivers a cross towards Iniesta and Messi inside the box, while Xavi takes up a position outside the penalty area.

 ASSESSMENT

Barca liked to double up on the man in possession, which meant that when they won the ball they could use this 2v1 situation to their advantage.

EXAMPLE 3

Diagrams 85.5 and 85.5.1 show the results of double marking again.

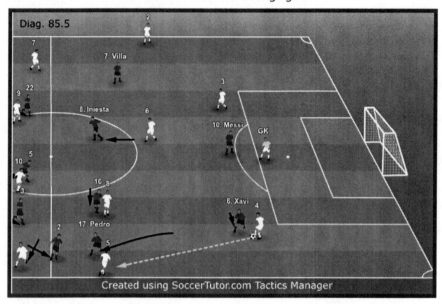

The double marking which is carried out on No.5 results in Pedro intercepting the ball.

Pedro moves forward and passes to Messi, who drops back to receive. Messi makes a run with the ball and either passes to Villa or shoots on goal.

INTERCEPTING A PASS FROM THE GOALKEEPER

Diagram 85.6 shows the opposition goalkeeper passing into the centre.

After the goalkeeper's pass, No.8 is being tightly marked by Xavi. Xavi wins the ball and moves forward.

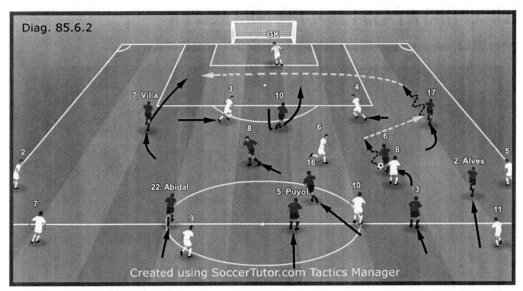

The phase of play can advance to a pass directed to Pedro and a cross towards Villa and Messi (diagram 85.6.2).

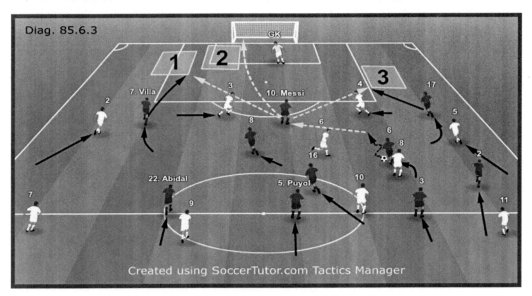

On diagram 85.6.3, Messi receives and has to choose from three options:
1) A pass towards Villa.
2) A shot at goal.
3) A pass towards Pedro.

CHAPTER 13
BARCELONA'S ATTACKING FROM SET PIECES

• Corner Kicks 274

BARCELONA'S ATTACKING FROM SET PIECES

Barcelona's average height (177.38 cm) during the 2010-11 season was the lowest of all European teams. This meant the team tried different ways to create chances from set pieces besides high crosses.

In cases when the team won a free kick around the box where a direct shot on goal was not possible the free kick was a short pass which led to the retaining of possession.

Corner Kicks

Diag. 86.1

When the team won a corner kick (diagram 86.1), there were only four players inside the penalty area (Villa, Pique, Busquets and Puyol).

Iniesta, Pedro and Alves took up positions outside the box, while Abidal was placed in a deeper position.

Diag. 86.1.1

Created using SoccerTutor.com Tactics Manager

When there was an opponent forward in an advanced position, the closest Barcelona player took over his marking (diagram 86.1.1).

The positioning of the players led the corner taker (Xavi) to cross towards the near post for Busquets, towards the penalty spot for Puyol or towards the far post to target Pique.

Villa moved in front of the goalkeeper hoping to get a deflection or to shoot after a header towards the goal.

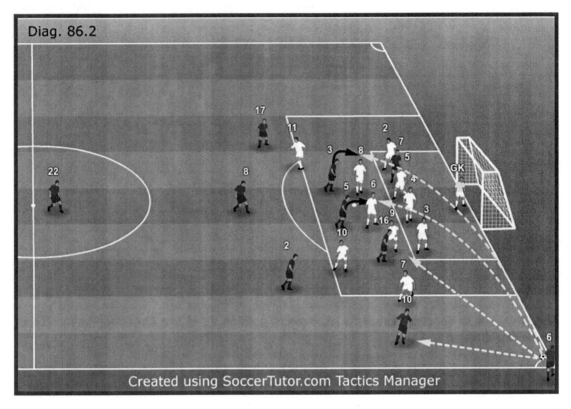

Diag. 86.2

Created using SoccerTutor.com Tactics Manager

In most of the cases the corner kick was taken by a short pass to Messi on the right or Iniesta on the left avoiding a possible loss of possession (diagram 86.2).

However in case of a corner kick taken by a cross inside the penalty area, the three men outside the box were ready to pick up a possible clearance by the opponent defenders and to retain possession.

CHAPTER 14
PLAYING WITH TEN MEN 278

PLAYING WITH TEN MEN

Barcelona are not the type of a team that use tough play during defending.

Therefore its players received only two red cards which were both in La Liga (Pique against Getafe and Villa against Athletic Bilbao).

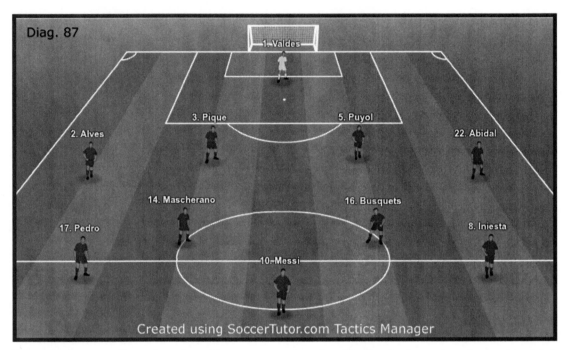

When the team was forced to play with ten men, e.g. against Getafe, the formation changed to 4-4-1. (diagram 87).

Leading already by 3 goals to 0, Guardiola placed two defensive minded players (Busquets and Mascherano) in midfield and the team had a passive behaviour, waiting for the opponents to come near the halfway line.

During the attacking phase Messi often dropped back into midfield to create superiority in numbers and to help the team to retain possession.

Despite the passive role of Barca during the defensive phase, when the team made the transition from attack to defence, the players fought to win the ball back immediately after losing it.

CONCLUSION

All the phases of play shown in this book set (Defending and Attacking) came from an extensive video analysis of the team's matches during the 2010-2011 season.

This analysis concerns the team's function in all of the four phases of the game and its aim was to show the elements which led to the spectacular and effective playing style of Barcelona.

THE KEY ASPECTS OF BARCELONA'S TACTICS DURING THE ATTACKING PHASE ARE AS FOLLOWS:

- The creation of superiority in numbers near the ball zone
- Messi's combinations and driving runs from the right side
- The creation of ideal formations (triangles and rhombus/diamond shapes)
- Maintaining width with the wide forwards and full backs' runs
- Synchronising the movement of all the players to create a cohesive and fluid unit
- The use of diagonal passes during the first and the second stage of build-up
- The use of vertical passes during the final (third) stage
- The use of diagonal runs into the penalty area
- The use of combination play to exploit free spaces (one – two's, cutting and overlapping)

THE ATTACKING PLAY CAN BE BROKEN UP INTO THREE STAGES:

The **first stage** which included mainly short passes from the defenders to the midfielders.

The **second stage** which included diagonal and vertical passes mainly by the midfielders to create a numerical superiority in the centre or on the flank. Defenders and forwards were also involved in this phase with the aim of getting into positions where the final pass can be made.

The **third stage** includes the final pass or cross to the attacking players and the final shot on goal.

The third stage was also achieved when possession was regained and Barca won the ball from the opposition high up the pitch, with many of these examples highlighted in this book.

BARCELONA USED DIFFERENT FORMATIONS IN THE ATTACKING PHASE:

• Against the 4-4-2 and the 4-2-3-1 Barcelona would make sure to have three defenders. Either Abidal or Busquets would join the two central defenders.

This meant that Alves was able to push high up the pitch into midfield to create a numerical superiority.

Barcelona would often have an overload of their attacks on the right side with Xavi, Alves and Messi linking extremely well in particular.

• Against formations with only one forward Barca were able to play with just two defenders.

This meant that Barca could use both full backs to attack and Busquets could also move closer to the attacking midfielders and contribute far more in the build up play.

Against all formations Messi would often drop deep to create an extra passing option and help create a numerical advantage in midfield, often 5v3.

We also analysed the tactics which were used in specific scenarios. This book manages to detail Barcelona's reactions to every conceivable situation, such as passing out from the goalkeeper, set pieces and attacking down the flank.

An essential part of Barcelona's attacking tactics was the extremely high level of cohesion between the players. If one player moved forward and out of position he was safe in the knowledge that a teammate would be close enough to fill in his position and restore balance and shape to the team.

It must be mentioned that the spectacular performances were the result not only of the tactical elements but also the technical ability of Barcelona players. For a team to perform well and be effective it must consist of players with the appropriate tactical and technical skills.

The most important contribution is from the coach, who must recognise his players' characteristics and adopt a playing style that suits them. From that point on it is necessary to have constant improvement individually and collectively.

The combination of these technical players and a great coach (and his tactics) have produced incredible free-flowing football and a lot of trophies. Barcelona are rightly described as ' A Team From Another Planet.'

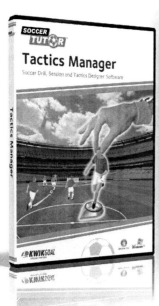
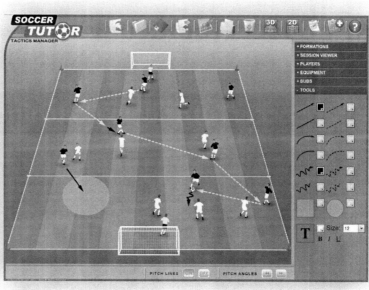

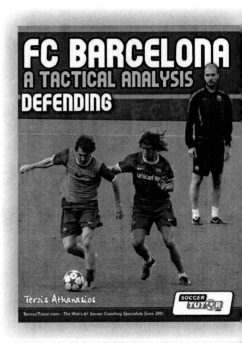

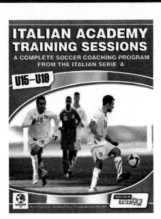

Lightning Source UK Ltd.
Milton Keynes UK
UKOW022007151012

200627UK00004B/65/P